The Confident Manager

Dream, Dare, Do!

Kate

The Confident Manager

Lessons in Confidence and Communication
for Successful Managers

Kate Atkin

*The Confident Manager: Lessons in confidence
and communication for successful managers*

First published 2008, Word4Word, Evesham, UK
Reprinted 2015, SRA Books

© Kate Atkin

ISBN: 978-1-909116-51-1

A CIP catalogue record of this book is
available from the British Library.

Printed in the UK by TJ International, Padstow.

Contents

Foreword

In my experience the successful people are those who believe in themselves. Others may have ability, but self-doubt can hold them back. Sometimes mistakes are made, and that's okay, as the mistakes provide lessons to be learnt. Too often I see potential in people who choose to continue 'playing it safe' even though deep inside they would like to risk a little. It's a lack of self-belief, a lack of self-confidence, that can hold them back. As managers they then fail to inspire others. To be a successful manger, you need a healthy dose of self-confidence, consideration for others and humility.

Often it is just a matter of waking up to the thoughts that run through your head to see if they support you in your endeavours or aim to trip you up. Reading this book will help you wake up to yourself. *The Confident Manager* is a book to benefit anyone who has ever had a 'wobble'. Experiencing self-doubt is what makes us human; coping with it and pursuing the goal anyway, while learning along the way, is what makes you great.

In this fascinating and highly readable book, Kate takes you on a journey of self-discovery, providing you with practical tools to boost your own confidence when you need it. I'm sure Matt's story will ring true with many readers. As his journey of self-confidence grows, so will yours. Although it's not just about confidence, there are lessons in presentation skills, quick tips for managing meetings and ideas on communicating with teams.

If you have already been successful in managing others you will recognise a lot of Kate's ideas. If you are beginning your journey into management and leadership, this is a valuable resource and a great starting point.

It is easy to fall into the trap of negative thinking when others around you are doing the same. It's a safe route to stay in your own personal comfort zone. Reading this book will inspire you to go beyond what you may have thought possible, to reach for those heights and, if at first you don't succeed, then try, try again.

I very much enjoyed meeting Kate and hearing her speak at a recent conference. Her address on the issue of confidence was very well received by the conference delegates. Many of them found it helpful to admit to their own fears and lack of confidence issues and to learn strategies to move beyond them. In reading this book I hope you will find the same.

Ruth Spellman, OBE
former Chief Executive, Chartered Management Institute

Testimonials

What people are saying about *The Confident Manager*

"At last a practical book that *actually* applies confidence and communication theory to real-life leadership situations. Whether new to management or needing a boost – this is essential reading."
Angela Peacock, Chair, The People Development Team Ltd

"There are managers, good managers and great ones – the great ones have confidence in themselves, but not to the extent of arrogance. This book shows you how to develop yourself to be a great leader/manager."
Martin Allison, former Head of International Banking Services, RBS

"This book does it! The simple tools to confidence all wrapped up in a story means not only an entertaining read – but the actual answers."
Walter Herriot, OBE, former Managing Director, St John's Innovation Centre

"I didn't think there was anything else I could learn about confidence building, but *The Confident Manager* offers a new view and new ideas. Well worth the read."
Mike Southon, co-author of *The Beermat Entrepreneur, The Boardroom Entrepreneur* and *Sales on a Beermat*

Acknowledgements

There have been many people to whom I am deeply grateful for their support and encouragement in writing this book. In particular I would like to thank:

Donna Beech, my wonderful completer finisher.

Sue Richardson and the team at SRA Books – for their encouragement and professionalism.

Walter Herriot, Billy Boyle and Simon Galbraith – for allowing me to pick their brains.

Andrew Goodwin, Keith Dheese, Keith Abbott and Clare Downie – for their technical insights.

My dear friends Angie and Catherine – for nagging me to write it and reading the early drafts.

In addition I would also like to acknowledge support from friends and the many teachers, clients and participants, past and present, who have inspired the stories and lessons.

To Absent Friends

Introduction

As Matt cycled to the office down the streets of Cambridge, the birds were chirping as if it was the first day of spring. For some reason, Matt felt exactly the same way. He couldn't seem to wipe the smile off his face. Life was good. He mulled over in his mind the tasks he needed to do that day – plan for the pitch to a new client, Spartus Ltd, and brief the team about Joss, who would be joining them on Monday. He wanted to get everything done so he could leave the office by 5.30 p.m. to meet Vicki.

That morning he'd woken up surrounded by moving boxes, packed to the brim. Tomorrow, he'd be moving into a new house with Vicki. They'd only known each other for six months, but already he felt as if she was his oldest friend. It was hard to believe that, in the early days of their email correspondence, he'd considered her to be nothing more than his Boston pen pal! Now, he was thinking about spending the rest of his life with her.

It hadn't always been so rosy. This time last year, Matt had been a workaholic, putting in long hours at work, while he ignored the gap in his social life. It was hard to believe how much had changed! Now, he had not only met Vicki, but he was making real progress in his new position as project manager.

Things had not looked so good at first. To get this far, he'd had to climb a steep learning curve. But the first thing he'd learned was something he hoped never to forget: there's no need to figure it all out on your own. Every step of the way he had turned to friends and experts for support and guidance. Although it had been

1

inconceivable to him at first, he'd gradually discovered that it was okay to ask his mentor for advice and it was even okay to fail – providing he learned something from it!

The experience had brought him a completely new perspective. As he approached the office reflecting back over the last six months, he realised it could all have gone very differently if he hadn't kept an open mind and been willing to change . . .

Chapter 1

Taking on a New Role

Six months earlier

Matt always loved his early morning ride through Cambridge. He smiled as he rode his bike to work, making his way between cars, narrowly avoiding pedestrians and other cyclists. The cycle paths in Cambridge were hit and miss, but he had worked out his own system for navigating the route. If only the world of dating were that easy to navigate!

Matt had just had an exasperating night. No matter what he did, he couldn't seem to devise an effective strategy for success in his personal life. During university he'd been dating the same girl – Paige, a fellow student. They had met during the first week of the third year and hit it off immediately. With Paige, Matt had never even thought about whether he was saying or doing the right thing to make her like him. Everything just seemed to work!

After graduation, they had both found jobs in Cambridge and eventually made plans to move in together. But then Paige got an offer she couldn't resist from a firm in Oxford. It was a turning point Matt hadn't anticipated. Overnight, the two of them found out how different their assumptions about the relationship were. Paige had assumed that they would marry and make plans to start a family. She didn't see any reason why they couldn't do that in Oxford just as well as in Cambridge.

It surprised her to discover that Matt had never even considered the possibility of marriage, much less a family. To him, the flat in Cambridge didn't represent the beginning of their life together, it was just a convenient place to live. He did want to get married and start a family, one day. And he admitted to Paige that, if he thought about it, she would certainly be "a viable option", but he'd never really given it any thought.

A week of long conversations and emotional phone calls had only taken them in circles. In the end, they had decided to part. Both of them were hurt and upset by the split. After several months Matt had tried his hand at speed dating, but it had proved to be a disaster. If he hoped to meet someone, he was going to have to acquire a completely new set of skills – interpersonal skills, specifically designed to make real connections with living, breathing human beings – and with women at that! Something far beyond the scope of the plans and specs that came so naturally to him.

Rewards for hard work

In retrospect, his break-up with Paige turned out to be a good thing. Having coasted through his job for nearly five years, Matt started to give it all of his attention. The loss of Paige suddenly streamlined his social life. Not only did he have more time on his hands, but he specifically wanted to stay busy enough that he didn't have a chance to think about his personal life, while he was waiting for time to heal his wounds. As a result, Matt poured himself into his job. His supervisors noticed what a hard worker he was, and he got on well with everyone in the team, always ready with a joke to liven up the day. He was energetic and enthusiastic about the technical aspects of the job. Not only did he come up with good ideas on a regular basis, but – without a girlfriend to go home to – he was always willing to work long hours.

James Pearson, one of the department heads in the company, started to take a special interest. To Matt's surprise, James called him into his office one day and offered him a new position as project manager. Matt was pleased, but also daunted; he wasn't sure he was prepared for the role. While James was describing the job, Matt was all too aware that a management position was going to require good interpersonal skills. His social life was already making him feel hopelessly inept in this area! Did he really want to find himself in the same situation at work?

"Your offer is very flattering," he told James. "But I have some reservations."

"The salary is more than you're making now," James smiled. "And when it comes to opportunities for advancement, the sky's the limit. You could even end up in my job one day!"

"I appreciate that," said Matt, feeling a little pressured. "But frankly, I've never considered a position in management before. I assumed I'd continue to work purely on the technical aspects." He wasn't sure if he should be so candid with James, but his anxiety was strong enough to make him blurt out the truth. "The thing is, management requires a level of people skills that I don't have."

James threw back his head and laughed. "I learned the skills to deal with people," he said simply. "So can you."

After many years at a high level of management, James gave most people the impression that he was a natural in social settings. His easy charm and finesse in interpersonal situations looked effortless. But that had not always been the case. "I was hopeless with people when I first got into management!" he admitted. "When I look back on some of the things I said to my staff back in the early days, I cringe."

Matt hadn't expected this. He'd never seen James look uncomfortable. He always seemed to know exactly what to say to smooth over any situation.

"We need someone who has technical know-how to head the project team. I know you don't have the interpersonal skills yet – but if you are willing, they can be learned."

James explained that there was a wealth of resources available to people who wanted to refine their interpersonal skills: libraries full of books on the subject, websites, podcasts, workshops, training, lectures. "If you take advantage of the expertise that's readily available, you'll build a collection of resources that you can refer to again and again. At least once a year I find myself looking back at a book I read when I was starting out. When I first read these books, I'd never even heard of some of the ideas before, now a lot of it is second nature! If you put your mind to it, you too can make the information second nature over time."

Ultimately, Matt would have three months to prove himself. At the three-month probation review, it would be much clearer what his managerial strengths and weaknesses were. "The review will give us an idea whether you are up to the job, and identify tangible areas for you to reinforce and to work on," James said.

James also offered to make himself available as a mentor within the company. "While you're getting started, I'd like to meet with you regularly to hear about your progress and review the things you've learned. Don't think of it as constant supervision; I have no intention of peering over your shoulder. I'd simply like to make my own experience available to you. Becoming an effective leader is an ongoing process. It's based largely on experience, but it also benefits enormously from mentoring. When I was making my way up through the ranks, I had some wonderful mentors and I'd like to feel I was giving something back by offering the same advantage to you."

"I appreciate it," Matt said, trying to appear more enthusiastic than he actually felt. "I know it will be a tremendous help."

> **You cannot teach a man anything; you can only help him find it within himself.** ~ *Galileo Galilei*

Early days

Matt had felt so elated by James's confidence in him that he'd taken up his offer with a sense of borrowed enthusiasm. He'd even wondered if he had been wrong to have reservations. Maybe James could see his potential more objectively. Matt began to wonder if there might not be as much to it as he'd feared. But soon, reality hit. His new role as project manager quickly turned out to be a challenge. He found Adrian, his direct boss, to be unenthusiastic about having an unskilled person in the role. It wasn't going much better with his team, even though there were only three of them. It had been his technical expertise and hard work that had got him this job, and he had absolute confidence in those skills; give him a technical problem, then leave him alone and he could solve it in record time. But now he was being asked to deal with something he'd never factored into the equation before: people.

Ever since his teachers had complained to his parents that he never looked up from the computer, Matt had tried to explain, "I don't need that fluffy people stuff!" But when James offered the opportunity to work as a project manager at a world-class company like Cambridge Enterprise and Design Ltd, he told himself it might be worth a shot. After all, what had he got to lose? It was just turning out to be a lot more hassle than he'd expected.

In the technical world, solutions to problems were more straight-forward. Once a solution had been found, it could be reliably put into practice again and again. People were far more complicated. Matt often found that, with people, it was sometimes hard to under-stand the nature of the problem, much less find a solution for it. And, even if he did find a perfectly good solution, it might not work the next time, if a person's feelings or motivations had changed. For all its complexity, the technical world was easier to navigate.

Although he'd been polite at the time, Matt was uneasy about James's offer to be a mentor for him. The week before, Brigit Reed, who had been one of Matt's closest friends since their days at university, had told him he should take full advantage of James's experience to learn as much as possible. But Matt was reluctant. He was glad to have the opportunity to meet with James, but he didn't want him to think he couldn't handle things on his own. Nor did he want it getting back to Adrian that he couldn't cope. "Besides," Matt had told her, "I don't want to take up too much of his time. James must have more important things to do than answer my trivial questions. If he promoted me to the job, that means he expects me to know what to do."

"I wouldn't be so sure," Brigit had told him. "Top managers often spend a lot of time helping and mentoring other people. They're not going to be around forever and they have lots of experience to share. What could be a more important use of his time than to develop others within the business? And he did offer."

Remembering their conversation, Matt grimaced as he rolled his bike into the rack at the side of the building and peeled off his rucksack. Helping, mentoring, sharing experience – it all sounded very touchy-feely to Matt. And it was exactly the kind of thing Brigit would say. She was very nurturing. It made her a good mother, but Matt wasn't sure how much of it could be applied to his problems as a project manager. He just didn't picture a man like James leaving space on his calendar for "mentoring others".

While Matt shoved his helmet into his rucksack, he noticed Roy, the guy from the HR department, strolling across the car park in a freshly pressed suit and crisp white shirt with a garish tie. Roy waved. Matt nodded back in response. In these early days on the job, he sometimes wondered what he'd got himself into. But at least they hadn't asked him to wear a tie! The jacket hanging on the back of his chair seemed like a fair compromise. When he got inside, he would dutifully put it on over the jeans and open-necked shirt he wore every day. Matt didn't like to admit it, but he was surprised to find the jacket tended to make him stand up straighter and look people in the eye. It wasn't exactly "people skills", but it was a start.

As project manager, Matt had to supervise a staff of three, present the work of the team to clients and interact on an almost daily basis with Adrian, his direct boss.

Outsourcing was the wolf at the door. Rumour had it that if their division didn't turn things around by the end of the year, senior management was planning to shut them down and ship everything to India. As word got around, people were starting to feel uneasy.

Thinking back to the conversation when he had been offered the position of project manager, he recalled that James had said, "I chose you because you're the best techie we've got. A guy who has talent like you can go far. I know you don't have all the skills you need to do this job, but I'm confident that you can pick them up as you go along, as I did. Your first task will be to turn your staff into a team."

Lowering his voice a bit, James had got up and shut the door. "Listen, Justin, Steve and Amy are all good at what they do. But right now, they're just sitting in their cubicles, doing their own thing. If you want any chance of saving this department, you've got to get them to work together."

Matt hadn't said as much, but he'd always thought that what he really wanted was to be allowed to do his own thing without interference – exactly like Justin, Steve and Amy. Now, those carefree days were gone. By bringing Matt in as a project manager, James was giving Adrian, Matt's direct supervisor, a fait accompli. It was already creating a certain amount of tension.

"What it's going to take, Matthew," James had said, strutting around the room, "is confidence, assertiveness and good communication skills. Let's meet on a regular basis. That way, I can see how you're getting on and be available to answer any questions that may crop up. Do you feel ready for the challenge?"

Eager to demonstrate his confidence and assertiveness, Matt had answered in the most self-assured voice he could muster, "Absolutely."

Sixteen days later, he wasn't so sure . . .

Lessons

Before his first Friday morning meeting with James, Matt thought back over the last two weeks. Normally, he didn't spend much time doing this sort of reflection. He liked to charge through life, solving problems and leaping one obstacle at a time. He was always looking ahead, not back. But James was offering him an opportunity that was too good to pass up, and the money was good too. Matt wanted to make a favourable impression and make the best possible use of their time together.

Who would have thought that he'd be managing a team? He still wasn't sure how the new job would work out and was starting to have some doubts. Because he hadn't been in the job long, he was really struggling to find things to say to James. He certainly wasn't comfortable in the role, and maybe James could help him with that, but he couldn't quite translate that feeling into tangible questions. It was hard to know what he didn't know!

Instead of creating a series of questions, he decided to make a list of the things he was starting to learn. If he mentioned some of these things to James, it might spark a conversation. He could always ask James for more insight into any of these important areas.

At the same time, Matt kept thinking about the three-month review. If he made careful notes about the things he was learning, he would be able to make a stronger case at his probation review.

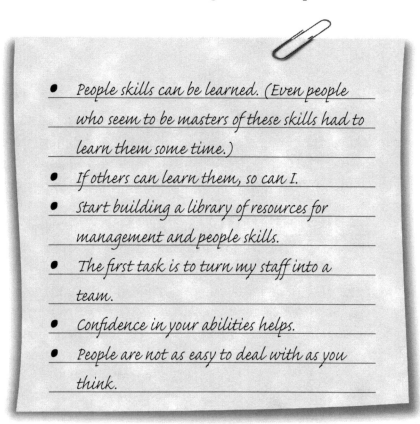

- People skills can be learned. (Even people who seem to be masters of these skills had to learn them some time.)
- If others can learn them, so can I.
- Start building a library of resources for management and people skills.
- The first task is to turn my staff into a team.
- Confidence in your abilities helps.
- People are not as easy to deal with as you think.

Chapter 1

Matt felt a bit uneasy about the list. What would James think? He might be struggling with the job, but he didn't want James to think he'd made a mistake in giving him this position! Maybe he should make the list sound more authoritative, like he knew what he was doing? Unfortunately, he didn't have time. The meeting was starting in a few minutes.

Surprisingly, James was pleased with Matt's list. Although Matt didn't mention his doubts about the quality of the list, James seemed to sense it.

"Self-awareness and learning come with time," James said. "Each week, you'll be honing your skills in observation. It's one of the reasons we're doing this. Recognising lessons and articulating questions about the challenges you face is part of the learning curve. You'll be surprised how much easier making this list will become."

Chapter 2

Matt's First Challenge

In the beginning, Matt had spent his time getting up to speed on the projects already underway in his department. But with two major deadlines approaching, it was time to give his team assignments, so they could give him the back-up support he needed.

In two weeks' time, Matt would be making a PowerPoint presentation to Millcreek Ltd, an important client that had been with the company since before Adrian, his direct boss, arrived ten years ago. Over time, they had gradually come to represent a significant percentage of the revenue brought in by this department. Matt assumed their business would be a sure thing, but since Adrian was going to sit in on the presentation, Matt wanted to pull out all the stops to impress him. He fired off an email to Justin.

> Justin
> Will you put together a 3-month trend analysis for Millcreek. I need it no later than the end of the week.
> ~ Matt

According to Adrian, Justin was a fast, reliable worker, always ready with an opinion, whether he knew what he was talking about or not. What Matt needed was data, not a blog. In order to keep Justin on point, Matt had assigned him the most analytical aspect of the presentation. The graphics, he gave to Steve.

> . . . Be sure to coordinate with Amy on the latest quarterlies and the projections . . .

he wrote. Then he cc'd Amy, so she'd be advised of what she had to do.

It was a relief to have the Millcreek presentation off his desk. Matt had never worked with a team before. Usually, the burden of gathering and analysing data or putting together complicated graphics had been on his shoulders. With a team to do the ground-work for his presentation, all Matt would have to do was present it to the Millcreek execs. No problem. He'd always suspected these managerial types, who got paid more than everybody else, were actually doing less work. Now that he was a manager himself, he could see that it was true. But, strangely enough, he didn't mind at all.

The personal touch

The only real connectivity most of the staff had with each other was online. If you had something to say to someone, you said it by Instant Messenger (IM) or email – even if they were sitting at the next desk. Text allowed you to speak in shorthand and get straight to the point, without the time-consuming courtesies you'd have to indulge in with ordinary conversation.

From Matt's point of view, email was also a lot more efficient than talking. In his Sent Box, he had dated copies of the assign-ments he'd sent to his team. It was useful for both follow-up and documentation. If there were any questions later about what he had asked them to do, it was all right there, in his email. If he'd walked over to their desks to tell them instead, he'd have no way of tracking what he said or when he said it and they'd have nothing for reference. It was an excellent system, but it had its downsides, as James had pointed out at their first review meeting.

"Project managers are notorious for sending a memo instead of meeting with someone face to face," James told him. "It's one of the first things I learned as a new manager. Dashing off an email seems the most efficient way. You don't have to get up from your desk. You don't have to wait till the person is available to speak to them. You don't have to write yourself a reminder note about what you requested and when you requested it – it's all there in the email. Very handy, right?"

"Right."

"But it's not the most effective way," James sighed. "I wish it were. But personal contact is far more effective. If you can look someone in the eye and tell them what you want, it has a much greater impact in the long run. Even if you can achieve your objectives more quickly with an email, you lose the interpersonal value you gain when making a personal connection."

"Even among techies?" Matt wondered.

James grinned. "Even among techies. I know what you're thinking: you'd rather send an email and you'd rather get one too. Why bother with walking down the hall and telling someone something in person, right?"

"Well, yeah . . ."

"Why don't you try it and see what happens? Send requests to your staff by email and deliver them in person. Find out for yourself if there's a qualitative difference."

> **What we have to learn to do,**
> **we learn by doing.** ~ *Aristotle*

Matt liked sending email requests for the very reasons James had mentioned. He couldn't help but think the efficiency of a two-line email far outweighed the needless effort of personal contact, but he was willing to give it a try. If nothing else, Matt knew that he didn't know what was best in these situations. His conversation with James had made him aware that his own behaviour could be an important influence on how well things went. For most of his life, Matt had assiduously avoided thinking about his own shortcomings. He'd always heard that "people never changed". Assuming that applied to him, too, he found it futile to dwell on any failings he might have.

James was introducing him to a new way of thinking. Maybe people could change. And if that was true, then maybe Matt could find ways of behaving that had a more productive influence on his team as well. It wasn't much to go on, but it was a place to start.

The idea of making personal contact with people, rather than texting them or sending emails, was something Matt had never seriously considered before. In fact, in some ways, he had tended to believe that technology had helped us "move beyond" personal contact. Text messaging of all kinds seemed so much more efficient than walking down the corridor – or even over to the next desk – to talk to someone!

The strange thing was, since he'd started thinking about making personal contact, he'd noticed that very few people in the company made eye contact as they walked the corridors. It was hard to get to know people when the culture in the office made it odd even to say hello.

Finding Ms. Right

Management was starting to suit him. He could easily see himself working his way up the ladder, buying a house, a new car and settling down. A few years ago such thoughts had never crossed his mind. When Paige left, he had put his head down and focused on his work. But now that he had raised his head, he realised he did want someone to share his life with. With the right woman, he could even imagine having two or three kids.

Meeting someone at work wasn't really an option. Apart from the complexities of office relationships, the culture in the company tended to encourage isolation. In the office, most people ate alone, quickly munching their lunch, while gaming on a PDA or chatting on the phone. Everybody's social life was rooted in the technology they held in their hands, not in the people around them. Matt was comfortable with that. It just meant that, now he wanted to meet someone, he knew he'd have to widen the net and maybe meet her online. So far, though, that wasn't going so well.

When he had first signed up to an online dating site, he'd created a profile that got no replies at all. After a week or two, he'd contacted the webmaster to see if his profile was actually showing up online! The webmaster had told him his profile was visible and his photo was receiving hits, and suggested that if he wasn't getting any responses, maybe he should consider rewriting his profile. (The webmaster admitted that he had never seen a profile that received absolutely no responses after two weeks.)

Discouraged, Matt had turned to Brigit. With her help, he created a new profile that started getting responses right away. It was an enormous relief. Matt had been unnerved to have had no responses at all on a dating site. It seemed a personal rejection when no-one took an interest!

"It's just the way you worded it," Brigit reassured him. "When you're writing a profile, you have to think about the people who are going to be reading it. What do they want to know about you? What are they looking for? If you only describe things from your own point of view, they won't be able to relate to what you're saying as well."

"Paige always did."

Brigit sighed. "Paige was special. A great girl. Very patient. Not everyone has that quality. Online dating is more competitive than an online job search. You've got to be at the top of your game to find the person you want."

Soon Matt was caught up in reading responses from girls all around the world. He had a brief email flirtation with a British nanny living just outside Bangladesh. At the same time, he started an awkward correspondence with a woman who said she was a physician working in a hospital in London, but she didn't seem to have any real medical knowledge when he asked about her work.

Chapter 2

Matt was quickly discovering that not everything was what it seemed in online dating. He tried to scale back his expectations, but with every new prospect, he felt himself getting his hopes up.

Meeting Vicki

Matt had recently started chatting online with Vicki, a financial services consultant working on a long-term contract at BMP, an international banking and investment company in Boston, Massachusetts. They'd quickly discovered they had a mutual interest in Imogen Heap and Sudoku. In the beginning, they primarily communicated by email, SMS or IM.

It just so happened that Vicki's contract was up in three months. She'd been debating about whether to stay in the States or come back to the UK. Her parents lived just outside London, but Vicki loved Boston and had made a good life for herself there. If she decided to stay, it was unlikely that anything romantic would come of this. Both of them had agreed from the start that long-distance relationships were doomed, but decided to be pen pals.

But, even though he hated to admit it, Matt was getting attached to her companionship. What had started off as the occasional note was quickly becoming an ongoing chat, interrupted only by meetings and time zones. Most days, both of them dropped messages to each other throughout the day. Some were longer than others, but they both seemed glad to receive them and replied as soon as they could. Early afternoon in London was the beginning of the working day for Vicki.

After delegating the tasks for the Millcreek presentation Matt grabbed his PDA and sent her a text on the way to the coffee machine for the last cup of the day.

> Made my first assignments to the team today. Feels good! I see why you like it.
> What's up with you?
> ~ Matt the Project Manager

Vicki had been supervising staff for years. Of the two of them, she had far more management experience and business acumen than he did. But he didn't mind. She never flaunted it. Most of the time, she just shared her experiences with him, as he did with her. Today was no exception. Within a few minutes, she replied:

> Just got in. Drinking my first coffee.
> Congrats on the assignments! Great to delegate, isn't it?
> Had the blues this morning because I don't know what's going to happen in 3 months. I'm worried, but there's no point in being negative. So I thought about what I wanted to happen, and decided to make it happen! Time to approach companies for interviews.
> ~ Vicki
> Here or in the States?
> ~ Matt
> Last night I listed the pros/cons of staying here or coming back to the UK. So far, it's almost equal . . .
> ~ Vicki

One of the things that kept Matt engaged was the way Vicki constantly introduced ideas he'd never thought of before. If they'd met last year, he might have been less interested, but his new job made her experience surprisingly relevant. Even the way she solved problems in her personal life was unusual. Make a list of pros and cons before taking a decision? It would never have occurred to him.

Lessons

At his next meeting with James, Matt arrived early, eager to get started. He knew he still had much to learn, but he was beginning to see that information really was available all around him. In fact, sometimes it seemed as if everyone he knew had good things to teach him! It was a strange concept to Matt.

For as long as he could remember, he'd assumed he knew best. Other people's advice had been something he'd had to tolerate from time to time, but usually, he'd found that his own way of doing things worked out best for him. Maybe that was true in some areas, but if he wanted to branch out in new directions, he was going to have to listen more carefully to what other people had to say and – even more challenging – solicit their advice!

Standing outside the office while James was finishing a phone call, Matt laughed at himself a little and shook his head. Every girl he'd ever dated had complained about the fact that he would *never* solicit anyone else's advice. He could be hopelessly lost in the heart of London, surrounded by people who knew how to find the store he was looking for, yet he would *never* ask directions. Now, here he was asking for advice about his job. "We're not in Kansas any more, Toto!" Matt said to himself, smiling. He couldn't help but feel a bit proud of himself for learning to take advice. It wasn't an easy lesson.

"Are you ready?" James said, coming to the door of his office. "Come on in!"

Matt's list of lessons felt more substantial to him this time. He presented them to James with a sense of satisfaction.

- List pros and cons when making decisions.
- Use personal contact whenever possible. Email is handy, but less motivating.
- Asking for advice is OK – other people are willing to offer help and it's a strength to ask rather than struggle on your own.
- Delegating gets things done faster and gives others the chance to be involved.

Chapter 3

Creating Confidence

Some of the things Vicki mentioned to him were so unfamiliar that they didn't really register at first, but her comments had a way of coming back to him at the strangest times.

When Matt stopped by the coffee bar on the way home that night, for instance, he noticed a poster on the railings outside advertising a workshop on business presentations. The edges were curling under the tape and it was peeling in the middle after getting wet in the rain. That meant it must have been there during the thunderstorm the week before. He came to this bar every day. Who knows how many times he'd passed it without noticing?

Going to a workshop was probably what Vicki would do, if she had an important presentation to make and had never done it before. It wasn't something Matt would normally consider. He'd always assumed these things were a waste of time, because he knew he would do just as well without them. James had also mentioned workshops though.

> **Man's mind, once stretched by a new idea, never regains its original dimensions.**
> ~ *Oliver Wendell Holmes*

Wondering what Vicki and James saw in this kind of thing, he took a closer look. Some of the words on the poster were blurred from the rain, but he could see that the workshop, Creating Confidence for Presentations, was being led by Kyra Radcliffe, a highly regarded corporate coach. Matt had heard her name bandied around the office. James had even mentioned it during one of their first meetings together. Up-and-coming management types were always quoting from her books, but Matt had never actually read one himself.

As he mulled it over, Matt moved up to the counter to place his order, but the cheeky barista didn't give him a chance. "No-fat, half-caf latte grande?" she grinned. Today, her platinum-blonde hair was braided with a long, pink ribbon and twisted up on top of her head. It was a new look for her, but her sparkling blue eyes were as mischievous as ever.

"Can't live without it," Matt nodded, putting the money on the counter. To the familiar sounds of grinding coffee and steaming milk, he pulled out his PDA, linked up to the wi-fi network and googled "KYRA RADCLIFFE".

The top three choices looked promising: two excerpts from her talks and a summary of the workshop. Normally Matt chugged his latte outside, but this time he took it to a nearby table and sat down to read. The barista raised her eyebrows, but kept any glib remarks to herself. Matt noticed, but ignored it. *You're not the only one who can do something new*, he thought.

The first site about Kyra had an excerpt on confidence. Perfect. He clicked it.

> We all need confidence. Depending on our life experiences, some of us have self-confidence in situations that others dread.

> Confidence is elusive. Sometimes, when we need it most, it's just not there. Other times, we exude confidence – even if we don't realise it. So what is confidence?
>
> - An inner feeling of self-belief
> - The knowledge that you have the information you need
> - The self-assurance to be assertive

Matt smiled as he read the list. Confidence was no problem for him. In fact, like most techies, he was often accused of over-confidence and even arrogance! Matt had always considered it a dividend of his work. Once you'd come up with an amazing solution that no-one else had thought of, there was no need for self-doubt. You simply tried out your solution to see if it worked. If it did, no-one could doubt your results. Confidence was a given. With a fool-proof system like that, there was really no reason to go to a workshop to build confidence. If self-belief, knowledge and assertiveness were what he needed, he should ace this presentation! No problem.

Matt was about to turn off the PDA and head home, when he noticed a link at the bottom of the page:

> **What Secrets is Your Body Telling?**

Suddenly self-conscious, Matt glanced around the room to see if anyone was looking at him. Luckily, they all seemed preoccupied with their own concerns. If his body was giving away any secrets, at least these people weren't picking it up! He clicked on the link anyway.

Have you ever noticed how your posture changes when you lack confidence?

How do you stand when you're feeling a little nervous? The chances are your shoulders are hunched. Your eyes are looking down. You aren't smiling. A worried frown may even creep upon your face.

All these physical cues send messages to your brain saying you're not feeling good about yourself.

And what does the brain do in response? It produces cortisol – a stress hormone that makes your stressed-out, nervous feeling worse!

The good news is this process is in your control. If you tell your brain to produce chemicals to help you feel confident, it can do that too!

How do you do it? Exactly the same way you make yourself stressed out – by adjusting your posture!

Because the brain responds quickly to your physical state, a confident posture really can make you feel more confident.

Go on, give it a go!

Tips for Confidence
- Sit upright with your back straight.
- Put your shoulders back.
- Relax.
- Keep your head up.

Without thinking, Matt pushed back his shoulders until they touched the back of the chair. It was an unfamiliar feeling. Hunching over a keyboard felt much more natural. If that's how he sat every day while he was punching the keys, did it mean his body was pumping out stress hormones all day long?

Making a point to keep sitting up, he scrolled further down the page to read what else Kyra recommended.

When you walk, walk purposefully, not hesitantly. Most importantly, never bend your head. Always hold it high. To convey confidence, it's essential to look the world straight in the eye.

Looking people in the eye was something Matt's mother had always been on about. The more she nagged, the less he did it. Since his friends at university didn't do it either, it had started to seem like something parents and teachers or other authority figures did. But now that he was a sort of authority figure at work himself, maybe he should think about doing it – especially if not meeting people's eyes made him look like he lacked confidence.

As he scanned the page, he saw something else he could relate to: smiling. This was one thing his mother hadn't had to nag him about. Matt had always had what she called "an easy smile". Sometimes he could get caught up in what he was doing and stay hunched over his keyboard for hours, but if anyone spoke to him, he always snapped out of it and gave way easily to a smile. It didn't quite make him a "people person", but he was glad Kyra Radcliffe was confirming how valuable a smile can be.

Put a smile on your face and *voilà* you feel better. That's because you're giving your brain a cue about how you feel. Your brain responds by saying, *"Aha! we are feeling good today!"* and so it gives you more of the happy "chemicals" that reinforce that state – serotonin and endorphins.

Often you don't even realise you're frowning when you become stressed or nervous. All of us do it, but we're so preoccupied that we don't even notice what's happening. The smile drops from your face. Maybe your brow furrows. Hormones, like cortisol, that create and maintain stress, start pumping into your blood stream. And if you keep frowning, your brain keeps sending the news throughout your body, *"We are definitely not having a good day!"*

Take a moment to think about a time when you were stressed or nervous. Concentrate on it and ask yourself this:

- Where were you at the time?
- Who were you with?

- What were you or they saying?
- How did you feel?
- What could you hear?

Picture yourself back at that moment in time.

Notice what happens to your posture, your stress levels and, in particular, your face, as you recall that moment. Do you automatically hunch your shoulders? Where do you feel the tension in your body? Are you smiling or frowning as you recall that moment?

Now let's reverse the strategy. Think of a moment when you just succeeded at something. Maybe when you felt the world was with you and you could do anything you wanted to. You felt empowered and strong. It was a great, confident feeling.

Concentrate on that moment and ask yourself the same questions as before:

- Where were you at the time?
- Who were you with?
- What were you or they saying?
- How did you feel?
- What could you hear?

Fully return to that happy, confident moment in time.

Now stop and reflect on what happens to your posture, your mood and, in particular, your face, as you recall that moment. Do you automatically straighten your back? What do you feel in your body? Are you frowning or smiling as you recall that moment?

What were the differences in facial expressions and posture between that memory and the first one?

My guess is that for the first one you had a frown on your face – or, at least, a lack of a smile – and for the second one, a smile came naturally. Your feelings would have been conveyed in a host of small ways.

Did you feel different too?

That's the power of your mind at work. Your brain simply does as you ask. It triggers the mechanisms in your body to correspond with what you're thinking. It looks for clues in what you're doing – whether you're smiling, frowning, tensing your shoulders or happily tossing your head.

So why not get your brain to give you a helping hand in feeling confident by putting a smile on your face? Yes, even force a smile when you don't feel like doing so! Not one of those teeth-clenched grins, but a full-on eye-creasing, lip-parting smile.

And, if you want to take it a step further, go ahead and laugh out loud – often! Most of the time, people around us are not laughing aloud, but don't let that stop you.

Laughter is contagious. If you start laughing, someone else is sure to join in.

Let yourself see that you are the one with enough confidence to get something positive started. Show everyone else how confident you feel and you'll start to feel it even more! Demonstrate how you *want to feel* with your body and your emotions will quickly follow.

Tips for Confidence

- Smile at people in the street.
- Smile at people you pass in the corridor at work.
- Keep your posture upright.
- Laugh out loud – often!

As he read Kyra's advice, it surprised Matt to think that he could *feel* confident, while giving off cues with his body language that made others think he *wasn't* confident. He thought they were just reactions to something he was feeling. Using his body posture to convey confidence to himself sounded like an invaluable idea.

What surprised him even more was the idea that he could have any influence over his moods at all. He'd always assumed that moods came and went, unbidden, and everyone was at the mercy of them, including himself. The possibility that he could do things to take charge of his moods was completely new to him. It was like one of those "Aha!" moments he'd often heard about. People always said those moments felt like a light bulb coming on. That's exactly how it felt to him!

If Kyra could show him how to control his level of confidence by sitting up straight or smiling at people – or doing whatever else she was going to explain in the workshop – Matt suddenly felt eager to attend! Maybe this Kyra Radcliffe could teach him a thing or two after all.

Kyra's workshop promised to cover something she called the PTP of Presence. Another link gave him a summary of the main points.

P – Posture

How important your appearance is.

How your brain works.

How your posture can directly impact your feelings.

You cannot have a negative thought with a positive posture.
~ Kyra Radcliffe

T – Thoughts

How your thoughts affect your feelings.

How to control your thoughts during presentations.

How to make your presence felt.

Why to avoid neutral language.

Try not. Do, or do not. There is no try.
~ Yoda

P – Pause

How important it is to allow others to think about what you've said.

How valuable it is to pause and collect your own thoughts.

How to allow others to think and answer – before you jump in and explain some more.

The right word may be effective, but no word was ever as effective as a rightly timed pause.
~ Mark Twain

Matt could see there was more to confidence than he'd initially thought. Maybe after these presentations were over, he'd have time to work on upgrading his interpersonal skills. He could consider it part of his management development training and James would be impressed.

With his first presentation looming over him, he really didn't have time to think about refining his game right now. Tomorrow, he'd get the data he needed from the team and start putting together the PowerPoint for next week. After the pressure was off and he'd brought in more business for the department, then he'd check to see if he could find a podcast of one of Kyra Radcliffe's Creating Confidence for Presentations workshops, or go to one in person.

Learning curve

Matt arrived at work early the next morning to start on the Power-Point presentation. Lying in bed the night before, he'd spent a long time mulling it over. After a sleepless night he'd narrowed it down to the key elements. As soon as his team provided him with the data he needed, he'd figure out exactly what he was going to say.

Matt knew there was a lot at stake, but the thrill of the challenge was starting to appeal to him. By the time his team started arriving, he couldn't wait to see what they'd come up with.

Justin sauntered in first, wearing his usual uniform of jeans and a button-down shirt. His long, brown hair was pulled back in a ponytail.

Matt was so eager to get started, he nearly jumped out of his chair. "Hey! Justin . . ."

"Hey, Matt," Justin said nonchalantly, tossing his backpack under his desk and heading for the coffee machine.

"Have you got those reports?" Matt asked, trying hide the urgency he felt.

"Hmm?" Justin muttered, rubbing his eyes. "Oh, yeah. I zipped them and sent them over around midnight last night. Should be in your Inbox."

Matt couldn't believe he'd been in the office for fifteen minutes without checking the team Inbox. He spun around in his chair and logged on. There it was, Justin's zip file. When he opened it, Matt found a beautiful, carefully researched analysis of the data. Adrian was right about Justin – he was fast, reliable and hard working. Exactly what Matt needed. Now, as soon as he had the graphs of projections and sales data from Steve and Amy, he'd be set.

"Steve, hi!" he said, the second Steve walked in the door. It sounded overeager, even to Matt. He could hear the anxiety in his voice. *Sound casual*, he told himself. "So . . . how was your night?"

Steve stopped in his tracks and looked at Matt sceptically. "Fine . . ." he said, dragging the word out slowly to emphasise what a strange question it was, ". . . for a Tuesday night . . ." He frowned a little, wondering what was going on.

Around the office, Steve spent most of his day plugged into an iPod, focused on his computer with absolute concentration. He was rarely seen in public without a gadget. What few people knew was that, when he turned his attention to human beings, no-one could make an assessment as quickly and accurately as Steve. It was almost uncanny.

It only took a moment before an amused grin spread slowly across Steve's face. "You're waiting for those graphs, aren't you? You can barely contain yourself."

"Well, no, it's just . . . uhm . . ." Matt stammered. "Whenever you're ready."

"I'm ready," Steve grinned, dropping down into his chair and pulling up a file. "It's all here. I'm sending it over now."

In seconds, Matt was opening the file on his own screen. Steve strolled over and stood behind his chair. "You new manager types are all alike," Steve laughed.

Matt heard Steve, but ignored him. The graph had his full attention. "Where's the rest of the data, the quarterly projections?"

"This is all I had," Steve said. "I was working with what Amy gave me."

"Where is Amy?"

"She's meeting with development this morning. She said she'd be here around eleven," Steve said. "What exactly were you looking for?"

"Well, not this!" Matt said bluntly, staring at the data. "These figures don't tell us about anything except a single quarter. That won't persuade Millcreek!"

Steve looked offended. "You didn't say anything about persuading Millcreek. You just asked me for the data from the latest quarter. How was I supposed to know?"

"Steve, Steve!" Matt said, impatiently, shaking his head. "You know we're putting this data together to impress Millcreek. What else is this PowerPoint presentation for? We have to show progress, growth – I can't do that with only one quarter, can I?"

Matt could see the pressure building inside of Steve. He looked like he wanted to start an argument, but instead he avoided Matt's eyes and answered, "No . . ."

"OK, then," Matt said, relieved. "Please bring me back what I asked for. The latest quarterly reports – from, say, the last three quarters." Matt glanced back at the report on his screen. "Are these the only graphs Amy gave you? Do you think she created them for the other quarters too?"

"I don't see why she would," Steve muttered, turning to go back to his desk. "Obviously, she couldn't tell what you wanted either."

A vague feeling of uncertainty washed over Matt. If both of them had misunderstood, then maybe Steve was right. Maybe his request hadn't been clear. He was sure he'd asked for the full details . . .

Justin stood leaning against a desk nearby, watching the whole thing with a wry smile. When Matt glanced at him, Justin smiled a little more, but didn't say a word. Matt couldn't tell what he was thinking and he was too worried about his own management skills in that moment to risk asking.

When Amy came back at eleven, he stopped by her desk and tried a different approach. "Apparently, there was some misunderstanding about my request for data and graphs," he began.

Although she was normally smiling and eager to please, Amy barely looked up. She seemed almost sullen. "Yeah, I know. Steve sent me an SMS while I was in the meeting."

Matt made a mental note to remind himself: news on the office grapevine travels fast. "What did he say?" Matt asked.

"He said you were incredibly annoyed," she said.

Matt blinked. "He spelled that out on a text?"

Amy shrugged. "No, but I got the message."

"I'm not annoyed," Matt started, then changed his mind. So far, honesty had worked pretty well for him as a manager. Since he didn't know what else to do, he thought he'd keep it up. The managers he'd known had been a lot less forthcoming, but Matt wasn't comfortable with that. He didn't think of his staff as pawns to be manipulated or employees to be kept out of the loop. They were smart, creative individuals, in much the same position he'd been in a short while ago. He was determined to show them respect. "Well, OK, I was annoyed, but I didn't mean to be. It seems I should've been clearer about my instructions."

Amy raised her eyebrows and tilted her head, as if to say, you're right!

"Amy, please let me know if you don't understand what I want," Matt said.

"I thought I *did understand* what you wanted," Amy snapped. "How can I know you want something different, if you don't say it?"

"Good point," Matt agreed. *Boy, this is difficult*, he thought. "You can't always tell if you haven't understood the instructions." He corrected himself quickly. "Or if my instructions aren't clear." For a moment, they seemed to be at an impasse, then Matt added, "That just means we need to stay in good communication with each other. I can stop by your desk more, to see how things are going."

Amy winced.

"Not to spy on you or hang over your shoulder, micromanaging everything you do, but just to make sure we're on the same page,"

Matt said. "And you can feel free to ask me if you do have any questions or if I seem to be leaving something out."

"I won't always know," Amy said.

"No. I get that. But we'll both be doing our best and that will help," Matt said. "Agreed?"

Amy smiled, tentatively. Her shoulders visibly relaxed. "Agreed."

Friendly support

When Matt told Vicki about the interaction later, she said she was impressed by how quickly he'd learned to admit he could be wrong. "A lot of new managers are reluctant to do that," she said. "They feel like they're supposed to be right all the time."

"If being a manager means you've got to be right all the time, I can't do it. Much as I hate to admit it, there's no way I'm going to be right all the time!" Matt said. "I can't really afford to pretend like I am. It feels like a trap."

"It is!" Vicki agreed. "If you can never admit you're wrong – or even that you *might* be wrong – you give yourself no way out. It becomes a terrible burden. The ironic thing is, no-one really expects other people to be right 100 percent of the time – not even managers. So there's no need to set yourself up like that."

"If your goal is to be right all the time, you're doomed to fail," Matt said.

"That's true," Vicki agreed. "Starting with the possibility that maybe you weren't clear enough makes it so much easier to reach your objectives. Placing the blame on your staff only creates resistance and makes it harder for people to get back on track."

"There must be times when you need to correct someone, though," Matt said. "If Amy gives me a graph that's wrong one day, and it isn't my fault, I need to let her know, so she doesn't do it wrong the next time."

"Yes, but even then, it makes a big difference how you say it," Vicki said.

"What do you mean?"

"When someone on my team makes a mistake, I like to start by asking what they were thinking," Vicki explained.

Matt had to laugh. "'Ohmigod, what were you *thinking?!*'"

"No!" Vicki said, laughing. "Not like *that*. It's like that old Confucius saying: 'Seek first to understand and then be understood.' You ask in a kind, considerate tone of voice, as if you assume they had a good reason for doing it like they did, and you want to acknowledge that."

"And what if they didn't?"

"Then, hopefully, they'll admit it. This happened in our office just last week. The paper vendor delivers our copy paper on Thursdays and this time, for some reason, he brought the wrong-sized paper. When we noticed it, I said, 'This paper would've fitted our old machine. Were you thinking of that one?' But he said, 'No, you're giving me too much credit. I just completely spaced out!' And then he brought us the right paper."

"Another thought," Vicki continued, "an old boss of mine gave me a really useful four-step programme to follow for giving someone feedback."

> ## Four Steps for Giving Feedback
> 1. Seek to understand what's happened and why.
> 2. Explain the impact of the actions.
> 3. Agree what is needed and what actions will be taken by whom.
> 4. Set a time to follow up.

"I like that," Matt smiled. "It's so respectful to assume they had a good reason. That's what made me decide to just admit the truth, when Amy said I was annoyed. I thought about trying to deny it, but then I realised I owed Amy more respect than that."

"Well, I respect you for doing it," Vicki said, softly. Matt noticed a slight fondness had crept into her voice. "That's not easy. It takes strength to tell the truth when you would rather deny it. It's hard to find men like that . . ."

Matt smiled, his heart warming a bit. "We aim to please."

"It's working," Vicki said, with a smile in her voice.

Matt found himself wishing she were in Cambridge. "I wish we could continue this conversation at the pub around the corner . . ."

"What's it like?" Vicki said.

"It's one of my favourite places. Very cosy. It's usually pretty quiet. And you can sit next to a big fireplace in the back. I think you'd like it."

"I'm sure I would," Vicki said.

For the first time, there was a quiet lull between them on the phone, filled with warmth and affection.

Lessons

The next day, Matt met with James. He had been exposed to so many new ideas since the last time they'd spoken that he was eager to tell James all about it.

"I've been reading a little about Kyra Radcliffe's workshops," Matt said. "I'm not sure I agree with everything she says, but she has some interesting ideas."

"What are you thinking of in particular?" James asked.

"When she talks about confidence, I'm with her 100 percent," Matt said. "She says that unless we take charge of it, our confidence is variable. Sometimes we've got it and sometimes we haven't."

"That's true," James nodded.

"She says confidence is based on an inner feeling of belief in yourself and that you can *feel* confident by adjusting your body language."

"Absolutely," James said. "Have you ever noticed Sydney, the guy who runs the file department and copy room?"

"Yeah," Matt said, picturing the blond, twenty-two year old with a gutsy laugh, who always knew where everything was filed. "He seems very confident."

James agreed. "It runs deep. Sydney strides through life like he owns the world. In the office hierarchy, he's at the low end of the pay scale. But this isn't real life for Sydney. In his free time, he's a half-pipe champion. He can do things on a skateboard that no-one here would ever dream of. And it gives him a deep, inner confidence that can't be touched by almost anything that happens at work."

"So the secret is physical confidence!" Matt laughed.

"The secret is knowing who you are and being proud of your accomplishments," James added. "It works best if those accomplishments are in the area you care most about – whether that's your work, your family, your fitness, your vocation . . . or even the half-pipe!"

"The physical aspect matters, too, doesn't it?" Matt asked. "Kyra Radcliffe says that your body posture changes when you lack confidence. And that you can make it much easier to think positively about yourself if you hold your body a certain way. Do you believe that?"

"Completely," James said. "If you stand up with your shoulders back and your head up, you immediately feel stronger. Breathing from the diaphragm helps too. It centres you in your body."

"The notes about her workshop had a lot of good body tips," Matt said. "I've never really given it much thought, but when I try these things, I do notice a difference."

"As your career progresses, you will have successes and failures. If you think positively and keep yourself on track, you will ultimately come to appreciate learning from both. Over time, the experience you gain will make you a stronger, more confident person. When that happens, you'll naturally stand up taller and speak with confidence. You'll shake people's hands boldly and convey all of these traits she's talking about," James said. "Or you can cultivate these excellent qualities beforehand."

"Choose to be confident?"

"Exactly," James said. "Present yourself with confidence and you will immediately *feel* more confident, as well."

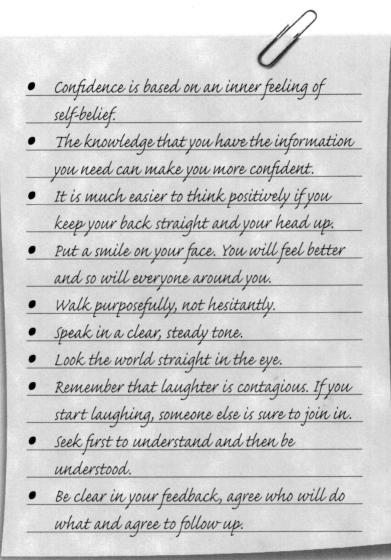

- *Confidence is based on an inner feeling of self-belief.*
- *The knowledge that you have the information you need can make you more confident.*
- *It is much easier to think positively if you keep your back straight and your head up.*
- *Put a smile on your face. You will feel better and so will everyone around you.*
- *Walk purposefully, not hesitantly.*
- *Speak in a clear, steady tone.*
- *Look the world straight in the eye.*
- *Remember that laughter is contagious. If you start laughing, someone else is sure to join in.*
- *Seek first to understand and then be understood.*
- *Be clear in your feedback, agree who will do what and agree to follow up.*

Chapter 4

Learning to Lead

James had quickly demonstrated how astute he was as a manager by giving Matt an off-the-cuff assessment of his team. Matt was sure that James had only had the slightest acquaintance with any of them, yet his analysis was extremely accurate. He'd managed to see things in each member of the team that Matt himself hadn't seen after working with them for weeks!

"Amy is very talented, and yet, she lacks confidence," James said.

"Amy is one of the best specs analysts out there," Matt added.

James nodded. "But when she interacts with authority figures, she's too compliant. I'd like to see her stand up for her own analysis more. Nine times out of ten, she's the expert in the room when it comes to analysis. But she acts like anybody around might have a better idea than she does."

"I've noticed that," Matt agreed.

"You need to help her change that."

"Me?" Matt was incredulous. How could he possibly help Amy with this, it was her stuff, he thought. At university, when Brigit started to doubt or second-guess herself, Matt had always teased her and reminded her of funny things that had happened to them both over the years. How could he do that with Amy? Teasing her like a college friend didn't seem appropriate and he hadn't known her long enough to have a history of business successes and foibles to draw from. Besides, why would his opinion mean anything to her? If your best friend gives you encouragement, you take it to heart. But if your boss encourages you . . .?

Matt had always felt a bit cynical about the bosses he'd had in the past. He'd always assumed he knew more than they did about just about everything. If they seemed like they were going to change his working hours or fire him or give him a raise – any of the usual things within their purview – Matt would have been concerned. But it was hard to imagine any of his past employers having much influence over something as personal as his self-confidence.

As it happened, James was the exception. Matt knew of James's reputation in the industry . . . James was an impressive guy. Matt felt a long way from setting his sights on such high achievements, but James's interest and approval did matter to him. He was one of the first authority figures, other than his father, that Matt had come to respect.

This gave Matt an idea! Maybe he could encourage Amy by telling her something James had said: "James agrees you're one of the best specs analysts out there," or something like that. Matt mulled over the possibilities in his mind. Since James was an authority figure, maybe that would hold more sway with Amy.

> **The difference between what we do and what we are capable of doing would solve most of the world's problems.** ~ *Ghandi*

"You are the authority figure now," James said. "You're in a position to give her the support and encouragement that will help her gain confidence."

Matt raised his eyebrows. The very idea that he was an authority figure in Amy's eyes amazed him. He hadn't taken himself that seriously. "Do you really think I have that much influence as a project manager?"

"You can," James assured him, "if you rise to the occasion. People want leaders they can respect and be guided by. If you are willing to take on that role, you can do a lot of good. Your remarks will carry more weight when people know you're taking your responsibilities seriously."

"Justin is never going to take me seriously!" Matt remarked.

"That's because Justin is cocky," James smiled. "He doesn't want to be seen taking *anything* seriously. It's part of his self-image to play it cool."

"He plays it well," Matt said, remembering how Justin sailed into the office every day, draping his lanky body sideways over chairs, throwing an arm over people's shoulders in a friendly, casual way. He was the epitome of smooth self-confidence.

"You may not know it," James told him. "But we moved Justin onto your team from the fourth floor because Fiona, his manager up there, couldn't take his attitude."

"What's wrong with Justin's attitude? He seems fine to me."

"To some people, Justin comes across as being very aggressive."

"He just says what he thinks."

"*Exactly* what he thinks – *as he thinks it*, without considering anyone else's feelings," James said. "You may not be bothered by it, but it can be very jarring. Other people have complained as well."

"Does Justin know it?"

"Yes, but he shrugs it off." James thought back to the conversations he'd had with Fiona to try and encourage her to help Justin.

"Of course he would." Matt was finding it hard to see that there was anything wrong with Justin's actions.

"I think you can help him," James said. "The very fact that you aren't offended by his bluntness means that you can get close to him without being put off. You can speak to him on his own terms, let him know when to moderate what he says, how to present things in a more appropriate way. It will work, coming from you, because you aren't put off by it yourself. You'll just be helping him realise how to interact with *other people*."

"And you think I should help him with this?"

"As project manager, you are in a position to cultivate the assets and develop your staff to build a better team. Amy will be a much greater asset to the team if she doesn't hesitate to present her ideas firmly and with confidence. Her ideas warrant that kind of confidence. Justin will be a far greater asset if he can learn to come across in a less blunt, less aggressive way. He can be an incredibly charming guy. If you could help him get his tone right, he could be a real asset in making presentations to clients. It's all about investing in the interpersonal aspects of the team."

"What do you think about Steve?" Matt asked. "I haven't quite got a grip on him yet. He stays to himself. He seems lost in his own world." *And he's also older than me,* Matt thought, but didn't say it out loud.

James nodded. "Steve just got full custody of the kids in the divorce recently."

"Oh, I didn't know about that . . ."

"In the past, he's been one of our best workers. Always on time. Always doing a good job, with enthusiasm. But in this year, while his marriage was falling apart, it was understandably difficult for him to focus. Adrian spoke to him about it once or twice, and Steve made renewed efforts, but now that he's got custody of two small children, he's even more distracted."

"Are you thinking about replacing him?" Matt asked. It seemed a solution to him.

"Adrian considered it. But I'm convinced it's temporary. Steve's a good man. He'll get his bearings. This is an unusually difficult time for him. So we'd like to give him some slack. But, of course, we have to protect our bottom line as well. Being distracted by his personal life is one thing, but if he begins to neglect his work, we'll have to let him go."

Matt was alarmed. He knew how upsetting and disorientating the loss of an important relationship could be. His reaction had been to pour himself into his work afterwards. But what would he have done if he'd had kids to think about? Steve was always adjusting his hours to take someone to the doctor or dentist. He sometimes got personal calls during the day that he had to take, as the sole person responsible for their well-being. Matt wasn't a parent himself, but he was sympathetic. He determined to do what he could to help Steve keep his job with the company, while he was trying to cope with his new life as a single parent. Though quite how Steve would feel with their age difference, Matt was unsure. How he would approach Justin and Amy he didn't yet know either, and he felt quite daunted by the task.

"Most of these issues won't affect you on a daily basis," James pointed out. "The most important thing is that you let your team know that they can come to you about anything. It's vital that they feel comfortable enough around you to speak to you about the small stuff. Otherwise, it becomes 'big stuff' very quickly. And that's much more difficult to handle."

"I'm trying to let them know that now," Matt offered.

10-minute meetings

The 10-minute meetings Matt had with his team every Monday morning always went well. Basically, these meetings were updates about what everyone was working on. They didn't even sit down for them. Standing helped emphasise the brief nature of the meeting. It meant, "We're going to stand around together for a few minutes and get the update." Once they realised how short and concise these meetings were going to be, the team seemed to really like them. So many of them had spent hours in long, pointless meetings in the past that the term "weekly meeting" filled them with dread. Shorter meetings were far more efficient.

James had recommended this idea from the start. "All you need is a weekly meeting to stay abreast of developments. Ask each of your team members to give a brief update," James had told him. "Make sure it's very brief. The entire meeting should last no more than ten or fifteen minutes. If it goes any longer, the meeting itself becomes cumbersome. Touch base with everyone, then move on."

At first Matt had found it hard to make the meetings just ten minutes long, but once the team got used to the fact that they were going to be simple briefing meetings – with no other reason than for Matt to give them a heads-up, inform them quickly of things and hear a line or two about their progress – the time fell into a ten-minute window easily. And the team seemed to appreciate being kept informed.

Matt was also discovering ways to get more out of their weekly meetings. He had learned, for instance, that if he began by asking for a progress report from each person and then spent a few minutes clarifying their mutual goals, he always came away feeling a tangible sense of accomplishment. He was hoping that all of his project management meetings would follow this trend.

Cracking open one of the books James had given him, Matt found 10 Tips for Effective Meetings. He was glad to have more pointers for the next meeting, as this one was to discuss the presentation.

10 Tips for Effective Meetings

1. Know the purpose of the meeting.
2. Draft an agenda and give others plenty of notice to add to it before the meeting.
3. Ask the right people to attend – too often meetings are unnecessary for many there.
4. Control and manage your meeting – as chair you are in charge.
5. Limit contributions to those which are useful and relevant – take other points outside the meeting.

6. Allocate action points and record these in the minutes (or if there are no minutes ensure people make a note of their own action points as they are discussed).
7. Circulate discussion documents well in advance to allow reading and clarification time.
8. Start and finish on time.
9. Allow everyone the opportunity to contribute.
10. Circulate the minutes and action points quickly (1–2 days) after the meeting.

Inspiring the team

Initially, Matt had assumed the preparations for this PowerPoint presentation could be handled entirely with a few quick emails. But after all the miscommunications that first week, he realised he needed to get everyone together. James was right after all; face-to-face discussions did save time in the end. He had hoped the meeting would flow as smoothly as the weekly meetings, but quickly realised that was wishful thinking.

From the moment the meeting began, Matt felt like the teacher in charge of detention. Justin, Amy and Steve pulled their chairs into a half-circle around his desk, then sat looking at the floor, like disobedient children waiting to be reprimanded. They'd been chatting and carrying on by the coffee machine a few minutes earlier, but now none of them said anything. They just sat there, waiting for Matt to speak, expecting him to be in total control.

Is this how it feels to be a manager? Matt wondered. It wasn't a comfortable role. He wanted to be the leader of people who worked enthusiastically together and took pride in what they accomplished. Instead, in the short time that he'd been project manager, he felt as if he'd actually undermined his team's confidence and split them apart!

Matt knew that Amy was a good analyst, but now she sat staring at her feet, embarrassed at having misunderstood what he wanted and providing Steve with inadequate data. Even Steve, who was normally so buoyant and sure of himself, seemed to feel unsure of the work he'd produced this week. It's hard to feel confident about what you're doing, when your project manager says it isn't good enough. Matt understood how they felt, he just didn't know how he could've handled things differently. *They didn't give me what I needed!* he told himself. *I had to tell them that. What else could I do?*

Only Justin looked as smugly confident now as he had at the Monday morning meeting. The analysis he'd given Matt was brilliant. But his success had driven a wedge between him and the others. Amy and Steve had pulled their chairs close together, Justin sat apart from them. It wasn't the team spirit Matt was hoping for.

For the next twenty minutes, Matt tried everything he could think of to turn things around. Being careful not to reprimand or embarrass anyone, he simply reiterated their goals for the presentation and explained again what he needed from each person. As he spoke, he reminded himself to use their names and look them in the eye.

When he asked if they had any questions, he was ready to apply the listening skills he'd picked up from Vicki and show them that he valued their opinions. Except no-one had any questions. They all sat, staring at their feet. Everything he said seemed to fall to the floor with a thud.

When he saw that it wasn't working, Matt tried harder. "The most important thing," he said, in the most inspirational voice he could muster, "is that we're all in this together. We're not supposed to be separate individuals, working at our desks. We're a *team!*"

They didn't seem especially roused. Matt carried on for a few more minutes in that vein, drawing on every pep talk he'd ever heard. Nothing worked. If anything, they seemed more annoyed and disgruntled than before.

Desperate to get through to them, Matt leaned forward, resting his elbows on his knees, and lowered his voice. Curious, all three of them glanced up. "Listen," he said, "you've all heard the rumours. If we don't bring in enough revenue this quarter, senior management is going to shut down our division." He had their full attention now. Each one of them was on the edge of their seat. Now he was getting through to them.

"I knew it!" Steve said. "Mark my words. We're all going to have to move to India before it's over. That's where all the jobs are going to be."

Amy put her head in her hands. "I can't move to India," she moaned.

Justin's first instinct was to focus on a solution. Very quickly, his analytical mind kicked in. "What does 'enough revenue' mean? What exactly do we have to do?"

Matt smiled to himself. *I thought you'd never ask!*

"First, we've got to make sure we include every bit of relevant data we possibly can in these two presentations. We need to bowl them over with our expertise, so they can't possibly say no. Millcreek will be a cinch. They've been with us forever. All we need to do is reassure them that they've been making the right choice for all these years. It's the second presentation that I'm more concerned about."

"Why?" Amy asked. Matt noticed that now that she was engaged by what he was saying she didn't have any trouble meeting his eyes.

"Because it has to bring in new business. Thegran is an electronics firm we've never worked with before. If we can put forward a presentation that wins their contract, senior management will sit up and take notice."

"We can totally do that," Justin said immediately.

"No question," Steve agreed.

"Then let's get to it!" Matt said. "You know what to do."

For the rest of the day, everyone worked full-out to gather information for the presentation. Matt had never seen such a high level of enthusiasm and motivation in his team. What had made the difference?

When he thought back over the meeting, he realised that the turning point had come when he had spoken to their needs instead of his own. The outcome of these presentations would have a direct impact on all of them. As soon as he demonstrated how this was important to them too, they were immediately engaged.

At the end of the day, Matt shoved his laptop into his backpack and said goodbye to the team. Each one smiled and waved, with a sense of camaraderie that he'd never felt from them before. *Now, we're all in this together*, he thought, as he headed out the door. He liked the feeling. Those few moments were his first experience of how rewarding it can be to be an effective communicator. It gave him a new feeling of confidence – not the cocky, ego-centred confidence he'd always had about his technical abilities, but a warmer, self assured, quieter confidence that rested in his connection with the others.

As he was going out the door, he got a text from Vicki:

> How was your meeting?
> ~ Vicki
> Great! I think we're finally turning into a team.
> ~ Matt
> Brilliant. Congrats!
> ~ Vicki
> Can't wait to tell you more. But I've got dinner with the Reeds tonight.
> Talk later?
> ~ Matt
> Absolutely.
> ~ Vicki

Chapter 4

Lessons

Meetings and presentations seemed to be constantly on Matt's mind lately. His conversations with James and Vicki, and Brigit and her husband Brad, had centred around these topics. He'd known there would be a steep learning curve on this job, but sometimes the changes made his head spin.

He kept thinking back on one thing James had said to him: "You are the authority figure now." It was a possibility he'd never considered. Some part of him still felt like taking the laundry home to mum or barging through as Justin did – just saying whatever he thought, as he thought it, without considering anyone else's feelings at all.

In his former life, that kind of lifestyle had felt like freedom. Now, he realised it was just a life of less responsibility. Imagining himself as a person who mattered enough to give useful encouragement and support to others was becoming more appealing.

He liked the idea that he could learn how to cultivate the assets of his staff to build a better team.

"People want leaders they can respect and be guided by," James had said. "If you are willing to take on that role, you can do a lot of good."

Matt still wasn't sure whether he could rise to the challenge or not, but he promised himself he'd do his best. He sat down and compiled his list to go through with James:

- Work **with** your staff to build a better team.
- Always know the purpose and agenda of a meeting before it starts.
- Manage meetings by limiting contributions, but allow everyone to participate.
- Circulate action points.
- Hand out relevant documents before the meeting.
- Start and finish on time.
- Be a leader your team can respect; honesty works.

Chapter 5

Dinner with Friends

Every Thursday night for the past few years, Matt had gone over to the Reeds for dinner. At university, Brigit had been his best friend. They had lived on the same hall in the dorm for the first year, then later shared a small Victorian house off campus with three other students.

Matt had never been comfortable around girls, but somehow Brigit was different. She had a very matter-of-fact style that put him at ease. Although he was prone to saying things that other people found jarring or blunt, Brigit never seemed to notice. They'd always liked each other and had so much in common that Matt had wondered, at first, if they might make a good couple. Brigit couldn't help but wonder the same thing. They'd tried getting romantically involved one summer, between their second and third year at university, but it hadn't worked out. Luckily, their friendship had survived. Just after they graduated, Brigit married Brad, a landscape gardener who quickly became one of Matt's best friends too. By the time they started having kids, Matt already felt like one of the family. Nothing could have been more natural than for Suzie and Alex to call him "Uncle Matt".

Thursday nights with the Reeds were often the highlight of his week. Matt loved spending time with them. He had assumed he'd be coming over for dinner with his own wife and kids before now, but that didn't seem to be happening.

"It doesn't just happen!" Brigit laughed, when he whinged about it for the thousandth time. She was standing at the island in their kitchen chopping carrots for the soup, while Brad poured Matt a glass of red wine. "Did you think the perfect woman was going to just show up one day? You've got to work for it!"

Brad handed Matt the wine, then he grabbed Brigit and kissed her playfully on top of her head. "Some of us have to work harder for it than others!" he said, winking at Matt.

"Some of us are worth it!" Brigit grinned. "So, Matt, what's happening with that girl Vicki? I like everything you've said about her so far. Do you think there's any chance she'll move back to London?"

"She's thinking about it," Matt explained. "Her leaving date is looming, so she has to make a decision soon."

"She won't look for something else in Boston?" Brad asked.

"Well, her mum and dad are here and she misses them . . ."

Brigit smiled as she stirred the soup. "And then there's this up-and-coming project manager in Cambridge who's looking for a wife . . ."

"I'm sure her decision would not have anything to do with me. She hasn't said anything like that . . ."

"Well, she wouldn't, would she?" Brigit smiled.

The thought that Vicki might be thinking of him when she decided whether to move back to London had genuinely never crossed his mind. Matt didn't know what to do with that piece of information. Normally, it would have made him nervous, but for some reason, it didn't. And the idea of Vicki living in London made him feel surprisingly happy.

Throughout dinner, while the friends were telling each other about their weeks, Matt's mind kept returning to the thought of Vicki. It was so easy to imagine taking her out to dinner, spending time with her on the weekends, even bringing her over here on Thursday nights. He knew she'd hit it off with Brigit and Brad. Funny how much things changed when he thought of her living nearby.

So much was uncertain. Vicki could easily decide to stay in Boston. Or, in fact, if Matt and his team didn't manage to save the department, he might have to go looking for a job himself!

"What will you do if they close your department?" Brad asked after dinner.

Coming out of the kitchen, Brigit plopped down on the sofa next to Matt. The kids roamed around the room, playing a game that looked something like hide-and-seek. Chippie, the family's lively cocker spaniel, ran alongside them. From the looks of it, he was not exactly sure what was going on, but was eager to play anyway.

"You wouldn't have to leave Cambridge, would you?" Brad asked.

"No, but I've spent a couple of sleepless nights about it, believe me," Matt said. "I'm just starting to see that I could really like management, I'd so hate to lose this job!"

"Really? You seemed pretty indifferent about it at first," Brigit said.

"I know. I was. At first, I assumed I'd just go back to what I was doing if it didn't work out. I didn't care much, one way or another. But after that team meeting I was telling you about, I really started to see how amazing it could be to rally a team around a project and motivate everybody to do their best. It was so gratifying!"

"You could always find another job doing that, if this one doesn't work out."

"Maybe," Matt frowned, starting to feel a bit anxious. "But the thing is, if this one doesn't work out, it will be because my presentations sucked and I failed to bring in business. It wouldn't be a great thing to have on my CV as my only management experience. There's a lot at stake right now for me . . ." He paused, then heard himself saying, "And for my team!"

"You're really starting to think like a manager, aren't you?" Brigit smiled.

Matt felt a little embarrassed. It was still a new role for him and he wasn't quite used to seeing himself that way. "I just hope we succeed. If we don't, I'm not sure what any of us will do."

Across the room, Alex suddenly fell down and bumped his head on the floor. At four-and-a-half years old, he got upset easily. He sat down on the floor and let out a long howl.

Brigit knelt down next to him and rubbed his forehead, then gave him a kiss to make it better. "There, now. It's OK, sweetheart."

With a little attention from his mum, Alex stopped howling and snuggled into her arms. She stroked his hair for a moment and kissed him again. Matt could see from the contented look on Brigit's face that she could have held him close like that forever, but Alex's mind was quickly moving on to other things. He wriggled out of her arms within seconds. Chippie was chasing a bright orange ball around the room. Alex ran after it, trying to reach the ball before Chippie did. In moments, he was back rolling on the floor and giggling, while Chippie licked his face.

Alex lives completely in the moment, Matt observed. *Whatever happened before – no matter how upsetting it was – is in the past. He forgets it and moves on and doesn't seem to worry about the future either!*

"Children switch between emotions so easily!" Matt commented.

"I know," Brigit said. "They're so spontaneous, it's always reminding me to keep my focus on what's happening now, rather than second-guessing the future or dwelling on the past. We used to know that as kids, but somewhere along the way, as we grow up, we lose track of it."

"We forget what it's like to live in the now," Matt nodded in agreement.

"Worrying about the past or the future just makes it harder to keep your balance."

"The thing is, there's so much at stake this time. If these two presentations don't succeed, I'll be completely out of a job." Matt was back into thinking about work again.

"Won't James find another place for you in the company?" Brigit asked.

"After I've blown the presentations?" Matt said. "I doubt it."

"You really think you'll blow them?" Brad quizzed.

"No, of course not. This first one on Monday is in the bag. It's just a renewal, basically. I mean, I'm putting a lot of data together to establish how good our service is, but they've always renewed before. There's no real reason to think that won't continue," Matt said. "It's the second one that will really require me to take my presentation skills to a higher level. It's a potential new client with a high-volume international base. I've never made a presentation of this magnitude before, so, yeah, Brad, to tell you the truth, I am a bit worried about the future and it's started to affect my sleep."

"I'm reading a book about this very thing!" Brigit said. "The author recommends making a Worry Box."

"A Worry Box?"

"Yeah, sounds funny, but it really works. You take a shoe box or some sort of small cardboard box and label it your Worry Box, and you keep a paper and pen beside it. Then, whenever you find yourself worrying about something, you write it down on a slip of paper and put it in the box."

"Like what?" Brad asked.

"Well, when I did it, the first ones I wrote down were:

> *What will they think of me?*
> *Will the kids be all right?*
> *What if the worst happens? How will I cope?*
> *What if it's brain cancer?*

"What if it's brain cancer?" Matt laughed.

"Don't laugh," Brigit said. "Every time I forget something, I say to myself, 'What if it's brain cancer?' I don't know why, really, but . . ."

"Do you know how rare brain cancer is?" Brad smiled.

"Yes, I know. It's not logical. But I worry about it, so I wrote it down."

"And how exactly does this help?" Matt asked her sceptically.

"Apparently, the act of writing it down externalises it, so your brain can rest and doesn't need to stay alert and keep reminding you of the possibility," Brigit explained. "You put all these slips of paper with worries on them into the box. Then once a week, or once a month, you sift through your Worry Box and screw up any pieces of paper that have passed their worry-by date."

"Efficient," Brad grinned.

"The really amazing part is that, when you look at how many of them actually came true – it's next to nothing! In percentages, it's like 1 percent of things we worry about *ever happen!* So by creating this box you can get them out of the way and go back to living life positively and confidently.

"When you go back to sift through your Worry Box, it's a great moment. If you wait long enough, a lot of your worries will have expired. So you can see for yourself that they never even happened!"

"Your worries expire?" Brad said, teasing her.

"Mine never expire," Matt said in a serious tone. "They're eternal. They'll be around long after I've gone."

"You know what I mean!" Brigit laughed good-naturedly.

"No we don't," Brad said. "Give us an example."

"Well, OK. Matt could write: 'I'm worried I won't do well on my presentation.' It's a specific thing with a worry-by date. Next month, he could take that out of his Worry Box and have a look and see that it never happened. He did well on the presentation and there was nothing to worry about!"

"Thanks!" Matt said.

"And then what do you do with them when you take them out of the box?" Brad asked her.

The Confident Manager

"Whatever you like. You can throw those worries away. Or have a ceremonial burning or something like that."

"With chanting and music?" Brad teased.

"I don't see why not!" Matt agreed. "What fun's a ceremonial burning without chanting and music?"

"Alex would like it, wouldn't you, darling?" Brigit said, as Alex and Chippie came running back into the room. She picked Alex up and carried him off. "Time to put on your pyjamas!"

Brad moved to the other end of the sofa and made himself comfortable. "Last year, I heard about some research being done by Robert Sapolsky, the guy who wrote *Why Zebras Don't Get Ulcers*. He was linking the actions of a zebra to the way the human brain works. Just say a herd of zebras on the African plains gets chased by lions and one of them gets eaten. If that happens, it's over. No worries. But what if they don't get eaten? What do the zebras do?"

"What zebras always do," Matt answered.

"And what's that?"

"I have absolutely no idea," Matt said. "The last time I was in Africa and saw a zebra on the plain was . . . never. What do they do all day? Polish their stripes?"

"They run. They eat. That's it. The thing is, if the lion is chasing the herd of zebras it might get one at the most, right? It can't catch more than that and, even if it could, it couldn't eat it. So, for a while at least, the rest of the zebras are safe. They go back to eating grass."

"Nothing else to do really. Have you seen an African plain?"

"They could worry. They could feel traumatised by the experience of watching one of their own culled from the rest and work themselves up into a flurry, too anxious to eat."

"They're probably thinking, 'Well, this is a good day! Aren't we the lucky ones? Isn't it good it was Polly instead of me?'" Matt laughed.

"Or, if they were like homo sapiens, they'd stand out there and fret, 'What if it's me the next time?' or 'Did you see that? The grass moved! Was that another lion?' But they don't, they're thinking, 'Right. Let's eat! We've got to continue eating grass and just get back to doing what we're doing.' That way, when the next lion comes along, they've eaten the grass and so they've got the energy to run away from the lion. If they'd stood there worrying, they'd be demoralised and they wouldn't have the energy to run!"

"Dreadful."

> **People are disturbed not by things, but by the view they take of them.** ~ *Epicitus*

"Sapolsky says that when we worry, our brain can't tell if we're right to worry or not. It just worries, no questions asked. So, if you're in a zebra's situation and you have a narrow escape, say in the car, and you start going over and over that narrow escape in your mind – reliving the trauma – the brain will release adrenalin and cortisol, the stress chemicals that can get you to panic and run for your life, whether you're really needing to run for your life or you're just reliving a time when you did. Before long, you're so stressed out, your body starts failing and you become sick."

"Those zebras should've written their worries down!" Brigit said, coming back to sit next to Brad. "It's supposed to keep your brain from constantly replaying things to be sure you won't forget."

"Whereas I prefer to whinge to my friends about how worried I am!" Matt said.

Brigit laughed. "Because we care!" she said.

"Of course we care," Brad agreed. "But whinging doesn't really help."

"Sure it does!" Matt insisted. "Whinging gets things off your chest."

"It's not productive. If you explain what's wrong, then ask for suggestions or brainstorm about solutions, then it helps to talk things over. But otherwise, complaining only makes you feel worse."

"It's cathartic!" Matt argued.

"That's what I've always heard too," Brigit said. "But it isn't right."

Brad shook his head, agreeing with his wife. "It's a myth. Whinging to your friends and getting their sympathy only confirms that there's something to be worried about. It makes your anxiety or discontentment more real. How is that helpful?"

"It's not," Matt said. "I'd much rather have a workable solution. Got one?"

Brad grinned at him. "No."

"What good are you then?" Matt laughed.

Brad shrugged. "I care . . ."

Despite Brad's disclaimer, Matt always found it helpful to spend time with friends. Their understanding and insights allowed him to see things more clearly.

Looking the part

A few days earlier, Brigit had spent an hour or more at his flat, helping him put together the right outfit to wear to the Millcreek presentation. As usual, she'd had a lot of sensible tips. At university, she'd always been on about his clothes – encouraging him to pay more attention to what he was wearing. It wasn't like he drew attention to himself by being unkempt or badly dressed, but Brigit always seemed to have a slightly higher standard than Matt did.

"Appearance is so important. If you look good, you feel good!" Brigit said. "Some people dress so they can blend in, others dress so they can stand out. The important thing is to find a way to dress that's right for you *and* appropriate for the situation you're in."

Matt had always felt jumpers and jeans were right for him. They were nice looking, hassle-free, and, until he started working as a project manager, they had always proven to be appropriate for almost any situation he was in voluntarily. (Weddings and funerals were the exceptions, but he didn't necessarily think of those situations as "voluntary".)

The thing about Brigit was she always knew what to wear. No matter what the situation, she had a finely tuned instinct for putting together the right outfit and making it look like it suited her perfectly. Matt was savvy enough to recognise this at university, but he generally ignored her advice about how to dress. It just wasn't something he cared about. Now, he was grateful to call on Brigit's expertise. She sat on the floor, giving him instructions while he tried on different shirts to go with his new jacket. "Even if you don't think it matters," she said, "what you wear has a subconscious impact on how you feel. Part of feeling good about yourself is looking good. An outfit can make you feel more confident."

Matt tucked his shirt into his trousers while he was listening to her. This was the shirt he liked best. It was a crisp white button-down, with tiny orange stripes. "I feel pretty confident in this," Matt smiled. "What do you think?"

"Try the one with the blue stripes. It matches your trousers," Brigit said. "You feel pretty confident no matter what you wear, I know that. But keep in mind your clothes have an impact on how *other people* feel about you as well. If you're dressed appropriately, they'll assume you have more credibility from the start. Now that you're in management, you should toss out any shirts that are frayed at the cuffs or any clothes that don't fit well. This is the time for a completely new look."

Matt wasn't so sure about the completely bit, but kept that to himself and resolved to keep his jeans and jumpers as well. When he had buttoned up the shirt with the blue stripes, Matt turned around for her inspection.

"Yes! That's definitely the one! What shoes are you wearing?"

He held up two possibilities. Brigit pointed to the black ones. "Be sure to polish them before you go."

Matt quickly buffed the shoes with the cuff of his shirt before slipping them on.

"No, *really* polish them," Brigit laughed. "Well-polished shoes show attention to detail. They make you look more professional. After you find the right outfit, you need to be sure you've looked after the extremities as well – your shoes, your hair, your nails.

Caring for every aspect of your appearance gives you a kind of subtle credibility that's taken very seriously in the business world. Even if people don't notice consciously, they notice subconsciously."

"Do I really care that much what people think?" Matt wondered. He didn't want to come off looking like Roy from HR.

"Your self-esteem comes from inside yourself," Brigit said. "But on another level, acceptance and approval from others can reaffirm your confidence and make you stronger. In business, you need people to accept you. If they think there's something off about your look, you may lose a client. So giving attention to how you look has very real consequences."

Matt slid his jacket on over the blue-striped shirt. He slicked back his hair with one hand and stood up straight.

Brigit got up and led him across the room to the mirror. "Have a look!" she grinned.

Tips for Confidence
- Clear out old, badly fitting clothes.
- Only wear clothes you feel good in.
- Polish your shoes.
- Check your hair and nails.
- Pay attention to the details.

The man looking back at Matt from the full-length mirror was a true professional. He looked more polished than Matt had ever seen himself look before. "I'm barely recognisable!" he said.

"That's because you're not slouching," Brigit laughed. She turned him back and forth in front of the mirror, so he could check his look from all sides. "And there's one last thing . . ."

"I know. Shake their hands and look them in the eyes."

"Good idea. But that's not what I meant. I was going to say: 'smile'."

Matt smiled automatically when she said it.

"Oh. Devastating!" she said, faking a swoon. "Your secret weapon. You can see the effect immediately," Brigit said. "A smile makes everybody feel good! It's not just how you feel, but how it affects other people. It's friendly and welcoming."

Friendly and welcoming was the perfect description of the Reed family. Whenever Matt spent time with them, he always came away filled with a sense of warmth. He wished he could describe that feeling to Vicki. He knew she'd understand why he liked it so much.

Fake it till you make it

When he left after dinner that week, it was close to midnight in Cambridge, but in Boston, that was only 7 p.m. With a little luck, Vicki might be home from work by now. Matt punched in her number on speed dial and gave her a call.

She was surprised to hear from him, but sounded pleased. They hadn't actually spoken in a week. Most of the time, they sent texts or instant messages back and forth. But talking with Vicki always felt as easy and natural as talking to an old friend.

Within moments, they were laughing and telling each other about their days. When Vicki heard the tip about smiling, she heartily agreed.

"I know exactly what you mean," she said. "Sometimes I go into a meeting with a smile – just to make myself feel better! I didn't know it was releasing chemicals into my brain, but I'm not surprised. It certainly feels like it."

"Remembering to smile, looking people in the eyes, checking to make sure they understand you – all of these things are so new to me," Matt confessed. "I've never thought about any of this stuff before. It almost feels like I'm learning to be a completely different person."

Vicki laughed quietly, then paused before saying, "I probably shouldn't tell you this, but there's a little trick I use sometimes when I go into meetings where I feel a little bit intimidated . . ."

"You? Feeling intimidated?" Matt said. "I can't imagine it!"

"In a new situation, where the people around you have a lot more experience than you do, it's hard to feel as confident as you'd like . . ."

"So what do you do?"

"You fake it," Vicki said softly. Matt couldn't see it, but she was blushing slightly. "If you're not quite up to it, you act *as if* you are – by adopting a role that's appropriate to the situation."

"'Fake it till you make it' as they say."

> **Many of life's failures are people who did not realize how close they were to success when they gave up.** ~ *Thomas A. Edison*

"Exactly. It's still you. It's not dishonest. It's just that, if you're not feeling confident, you think about what a confident person would do and then act as if you are that someone!"

"Does it work?"

"It's astounding how well it works," Vicki said. "People do it all the time. A lot of the confident people around us are just acting. They act *as if* they are full of confidence and, before long, they find themselves creating the real thing inside themselves. Sometimes, the people we think of as extremely confident, who seem to have a greater sense of self-belief than anyone else has in them, are just acting."

"The thing is, I am truly confident when it comes to my work," Matt explained. "I'm not faking it at all. I know I'm good at what I do, so why shouldn't I be confident? My results speak for themselves. But in this project management position, the rules are different. I'm not even sure I always know what they are!"

"That's how I felt when I first started out in management too," Vicki said. "I wanted to dress and behave appropriately, but I didn't have any models in my life to go by."

"What did you do?"

"I used a role model from TV!" Vicki laughed. "At the time, there was this TV show about powerful female attorneys in a law firm. It was a completely different type of business, but I liked their style. They were strong and direct and almost impossibly confident. I thought, 'I could use a little of that!'

"Then, one day, when I was in a situation at work where I needed to feel strong and direct, but I wasn't sure how to do it, I found myself remembering this attorney from the show. And, for that meeting, I just adopted her role in my head."

"Did anyone notice you were doing her?" Matt asked.

"Well, it's not like I was impersonating her voice or anything," Vicki laughed. "I just used her confident style as a model. So I think everyone saw a stronger, more confident me. The meeting went much better anyway . . ."

"Have you done it since?"

"Until I really internalised a more confident style, I used it all the time. After it worked so well at that first meeting, I watched the character on the TV show more closely. I thought carefully about what she was doing that made her seem so confident – what words did she use? How did she behave? When you pay close attention, you can see all kinds of small actions that convey strength and confidence, not just the more obvious ones. It really works!"

Adopt a role

When you are feeling unsure about what to do and worrying about how you'll be perceived, why not adopt a role that makes you feel more confident?

If you don't start speaking with a different accent or behaving like a lunatic, no-one else will even know. You'll simply come across with more poise and certainty. Sometimes, if you're feeling insecure, the sound of your own voice speaking with authority can be very reassuring.

Suppose yourself to be a person you admire who would handle this nerve-wracking situation easily. (The chances are good that that person has moments of insecurity too. But no matter. As far as you're concerned, they would barely find this situation to be a challenge. So if you emulate them, you'll be on firm footing.)

One thing's certain: confidence breeds confidence. The more confident you sound, the more confident you'll feel. The more confidence you convey, the more other people will react to you with respect and confidence, which will make you feel more confident as well. Why soak in anxiety, when you can get a confidence feedback loop going?!

Have you ever observed that if you enter a room with your head high, a smile on your face and a steady, confident stride, people take notice? Adopting the role of a justifiably confident person immediately affects the way you enter a room. The interested reactions of the people in the room will help you hold that confidence in place.

In a demanding social situation, it's sometimes useful to adopt the role of "host". Rather than being intimidated by a room full of executives and feeling like a wallflower, it's much better to cast yourself in the role of the host or hostess. Be the one to introduce people to others. It will rid you of the passive feeling that others should be coming to you. Once this feeling has time to simmer, it can easily turn into worry and anxiety that they are *not* coming to you! Choose a stronger position for yourself.

If you adopt the role of host, you'll put aside your own reservations and start thinking about other people, making introductions. At the same time, you'll be seen to be in charge. Offer drinks to those around you. Help serve the food if you're at a social function. In a work situation, this role is even more important. The smallest cog in the biggest wheel has an important role to play.

If you have a crisis, your role can come in very handy. It can help you separate yourself from the crisis. If, for example, your boss or your client gets angry, it will be easier to remember that their reaction is not personal; it is directed towards the role you're playing. Their anger is towards your position, towards something you did in your role or towards an action your company has taken. It's not about you.

As you go through the course of your day, at home and at work, start noticing the times when you feel most uneasy. What kinds of situations challenge you most? In what settings do you feel less confident? What kind of role could make those situations easier for you?

Perhaps you are nervous about being in a new management position, when you still think of yourself as junior. Visualising the ultimate manager, then adopting that role for yourself, can really help ease your transition. As you take actions and make choices that validate your success as a manager, you gradually come to realise that you have made that role a reality. You are no longer a junior, pretending to be a good manager. You really are a good manager and your actions prove it.

Keep these things in mind as you adopt a greater level of confidence.

> **Tips for Confidence**
> - Act as if you are confident.
> - Find a confident role model.
> - Look for words and small actions that convey confidence.
> - Fake it till you make it.

Lessons

When he returned to his notes about the lessons he'd been learning lately, Matt was surprised to realise how much valuable advice he'd got from Brigit and Brad. He always valued their input on his personal life, of course, but he'd never imagined that their family would make such a contribution to his professional growth too! This week, even Alex had been a sage in his own way.

Matt was prone to worry a problem to death. Sometimes it would take him a while to notice there was a problem – especially when it had to do with social issues. Once he recognised it, though, he had a tendency to over-analyse it.

But that wasn't the worst of it! After he'd made a decision, he could waste a remarkable amount of energy second-guessing it. *Maybe I should've made the other choice* was a thought that often plagued him. He was sure Kyra Radcliffe would say he was indulging in negative thinking. No doubt his shoulders were slumped at the time, as well!

Matt thought back to dinner at the Reeds. With one jubilant burst through the room, Alex had demonstrated a completely different way of life. Nothing existed for him but the present moment. From time to time he might remember that his mother had promised to take him to the park or his dad had said they'd play ball on the weekend, but those dates and times existed on the fringes of his reality. Primarily, he lived in the Now. Like most children, he was the embodiment of spontaneity.

Pulling his list together for James, Matt reviewed how much he had taken on board and changed recently.

- *Worrying about the past or the future just makes it harder to keep your balance.*
- *Create a Worry Box, so your brain can rest and stop reminding you about your worries.*
- *Check on your worries later to see how few of them have actually happened.*
- *Remember: zebras never worry. They don't have to. And neither do you.*
- *The brain creates chemicals based on thoughts and posture – not on reality.*

- Appearance is vital. If you look good, you feel good.
- Dress in a way that's right for you **and** the situation. Only wear clothes you feel good in.
- Pay attention to the details: polish your shoes, check your hair and nails.
- Act **as if** you are confident.
- Fake it till you make it.

Chapter 6

Making the Presentation

On the morning of the presentation, Matt woke up at 5 a.m. to review his notes. He couldn't count the number of times he'd rehearsed his words to the PowerPoint slides over the past few days, but it couldn't hurt to run through it one more time. As he clicked over the slides, he reminded himself silently of what he was going to say.

Every time he went through it he felt better about his chances of success. This was a great presentation. The data was strong, the graphs were vivid. Once he had made more effective efforts to communicate his intentions to his team, they had each provided him with very persuasive material. He couldn't help but feel proud of them – and of himself as well. As long as he didn't make any appalling errors delivering it, he believed the client should be more than happy to renew their contract.

Thanks to all the tips he'd been getting, Matt felt more comfortable putting on his business outfit and adopting a confident, professional role. As Vicki had suggested, he'd picked out a character from a TV show he especially liked and decided to walk and talk like that character, as much as possible, whenever he started to feel any doubts creep in. Just imagining that character made him stand taller and hold his chin a certain way. Matt couldn't help but smile. He liked the feeling!

For the final touches, Matt polished his shoes and pulled on his jacket, then stood in front of the mirror, checking himself out from different angles. He couldn't remember ever doing this before a meeting in the past. It was something Brigit had encouraged. And it was a good thing too. This morning, when he checked his reflection from behind, he noticed the bottom of his jacket was turned up! What if he'd walked into the meeting like that? It wouldn't be the end of the world, of course, but he did want to look his best. And he was starting to realise Brigit was right: attention to detail really matters.

That's why he wanted to be waiting at the office when Adrian arrived. The two of them were going to go to Millcreek in Adrian's car, but Matt wanted to demonstrate his readiness and professionalism by being there early. When he arrived at the office at 7.45 a.m., Adrian had not got in yet. Matt smoothed down his hair one more time. This day was right on track. He had a good feeling about it.

"You're here early, Matthew!" Adrian's voice boomed through the empty corridor. "Feeling nervous?" he smirked.

"Feeling confident," Matt replied, releasing those feel-good chemicals into his brain with a broad smile.

The two men made uneasy small talk on the way to the Millcreek building. Matt could tell that Adrian was still somewhat resentful that James had superseded his authority by making Matt project manager. He wasn't sure how far that resentment went. Did Adrian actually hope he'd fail?

If the department was shut down, Adrian would still have a job. So he had less at stake in this presentation than Matt did. If Matt succeeded, he would look good too. If Matt failed, he could say James was wrong. Either way, it was a win/win situation for Adrian.

He should have been happy, but he seemed tense and irascible instead. From what Matt could tell, Adrian was always in a tense, irascible mood.

Before they'd even arrived at Millcreek, negative thoughts were beginning to creep into Matt's mind. *Adrian is hoping I'll fall flat on my face,* he told himself. When he tried to guess what Adrian was thinking, this was only one of several possibilities. But in that moment of anxiety, this negative scenario felt the most likely to Matt. *While I'm up there, feeling nervous and trying to do my best, he's going to be silently finding fault with what I'm doing. He'd be only too happy to see me fail. There's no way for me to be good enough to please him.*

Matt sighed and leant his head back against the seat of the car. If he could just get through this day and keep Millcreek's business, he could put all this anxiety behind him.

When Adrian pulled the car into the car park, Matt was surprised to see that Millcreek was located in one of the most impressive buildings he'd ever seen. He'd assumed it would be in a relatively small industrial park, not a sophisticated glass monolith like this. The high rise represented the latest contemporary architecture in the city. And it turned out that Millcreek owned the building. Matt started to feel more intimidated than ever. *These people are completely out of your league,* his mind chattered. *If this presentation hinges on you, it's doomed.*

In the lobby, the glass walls rose up at least five floors with escalators taking people to the upper floors. With so many people in suits scurrying around, Matt couldn't help but think of ants, going about their business in a glass ant farm. The magnitude of the scale was overwhelming.

Millcreek, naturally, was on the top floor. An enormous reception desk extended in an arc around the room. It was longer than Matt's entire kitchen. At the opposite end of the room a rugged slate wall rose up about nine feet. Streaming down the slate was a perpetual waterfall. It splashed into a rectangular stone pond at the base, making a gentle sloshing sound that Matt found soothing. In an intimidating environment like this he could see why they'd need a reassuring water feature in the waiting room.

Matt took solace in the sound, but he didn't have long to enjoy it.

"Sorry to keep you waiting." A poised, impeccably dressed assistant greeted Matt and Adrian with a notebook in her hands. "I'm Suri Ramta. Everyone's ready for your presentation, but we've got two more to fit in this morning. I know we said you'd have thirty minutes, but is there any way you could shorten it to fifteen? That's really all the time we have."

"Of course," Adrian smiled, without glancing at Matt.

> **The human brain starts working the moment you are born and never stops until you stand up to speak in public.** ~ *George Jessel*

Suddenly, Matt could feel his heart beating in his chest. It was picking up speed. *Fifteen minutes?* Adrian hadn't even mentioned the thirty-minute cut-off. Matt had had no idea they'd be on such a tight schedule. There was a lot of information to cover in fifteen minutes. *Could he do it?*

If only he had a little time to go over the material again and come up with a way to shorten it, but as soon as they stepped into the boardroom, he could see that wouldn't be possible. Four Millcreek executives were already waiting around the table. It was obvious from their expressions that they didn't have time to waste.

Brigit would have been disappointed – they weren't even wearing jackets! One of them had brought a jacket, apparently, but he'd already tossed it over the back of a nearby chair. What Matt noticed first was how confident and sophisticated they all looked. The entire atmosphere in the room was charged with that same energy.

Fake it till you make it! Matt reminded himself, drawing on his TV role model. He quickly moved to the lectern and started setting up his equipment. As he expected, Millcreek's facilities were state of the art. There was a backlit screen on the wall and an infrared touch panel for the projector. All he had to do was hook his laptop up and the wi-fi connection sent his PowerPoint slides to the screen.

The only thing he needed was more elbowroom. However sleek and modern it might be, the room was uncomfortably small for seven adults. It felt like they were almost on top of one another. When Matt's first slide appeared on the screen, he realised that the man sitting next to him was actually close enough to see his notes!

It wasn't the best situation, but the clock was ticking. Matt glanced quickly at his watch. It was 10.45. That meant he had until 11.00. It was a lot to accomplish, but he could do it if he hurried. Matt turned on the projector and starting whizzing through the slides. The only way he was going to get everything in was to start talking as fast as he could!

Matt tried to pace the slides evenly over the allotted fifteen minutes and was quite pleased with himself when he hurried through the last few graphs, just as his watch clicked to 11.00. Not many people could have covered such complicated information in such a small window of time. He smiled a little smugly as he turned back around to face the room.

What he saw was not what he expected. Instead of smiling faces, sharing his impression that he'd done an amazing job, Matt noticed the executives at Millcreek exchanging unhappy glances. Adrian actually looked angry and tense. Matt couldn't understand what was going on. The data was absolutely accurate. It had come directly from the research and testing department, which was always very precise in its evaluations. There was no reason to question anything he'd said and all of his slides pointed to positive developments that Millcreek could take advantage of by renewing their contract. It was all good news! What could have gone wrong?

Suri Ramta rose from her chair and thanked Matt politely for coming. But there was a chill in the air. Adrian looked like he wanted to say something to Ramta, to apologise or explain, but he resisted the urge and shook the executives' hands with resignation.

When they left the building, he vented his exasperation on Matt instead. "What on earth were you thinking?!" Adrian exclaimed, as they crossed the car park together and got into the car.

"What do you mean?" Matt said. It was obvious something had gone badly wrong, but he wasn't sure of the best way to handle this situation. He didn't want to look Adrian in the eye. If only he knew what had gone wrong, he could explain it or defend himself. Instead, he felt lost. "I thought it went well. The data was solid. I finished on time . . ."

"You finished at the speed of light!" Adrian said.

"Well, they only gave us fifteen minutes . . ."

"So you should have eliminated something, instead of trying to cram it all in! How were they supposed to process that much information?"

For a moment, Matt thought about what it must have been like to be an executive sitting at the table, with an expert flashing through the slides and speaking as fast as he could to get in all of the details.

"If you'd turned around, you would've noticed their body language," Adrian sighed. "Ramta folded her arms and started looking at her watch within the first five minutes. No-one was paying attention as you rattled off that data. The looks in their eyes would've told you that, but you kept your back to the room the whole time! I couldn't believe it."

"Yeah, I was just thinking about getting through all the slides, so I –"

"You took your eyes off the ball. We weren't there to make them the best-informed executives on the planet. We were there to persuade them to renew their contract," Adrian said. "What we needed to do was make them *want it* – not keep them informed about the latest developments."

He didn't tell Adrian, but Matt had assumed that if the Millcreek executives knew about the latest developments, they *would* want to renew their contract. It was only logical.

"You never considered them at all, did you? Nothing you said took their point of view into consideration. You gave them the facts, but we could have sent them that information in a manual. What they needed to hear was something that reached them where they lived, that let them know what we can do for them. You never talked about that. You didn't even answer their questions."

"They had questions?" Now Matt was really surprised. *How could I have missed that?*

"They might have!" Adrian said, exasperated. "How would you know? You didn't ask."

Matt felt annoyed. "I'm sorry, but they cut our time in half. I barely had time to cover the important points, much less to take questions!"

"It would have been better to give them five minutes of information about what we can do for them, then open the floor to questions, than to rush through irrelevant data for fifteen minutes."

"It wasn't irrelevant!"

"If you don't find a way to make it relevant to them, it might as well be irrelevant!" Adrian was shaking his head. "Your presentation skills need a lot more work than I expected. I know James wants you to head up this department, but maybe we should think about getting someone from sales to make the presentation next week . . ."

"No!" Matt said, earnestly. "I can do this. I've been talking to people all week about presentation skills and I just need a little time to get up to speed. I may have blown this one but, trust me, I'll do much better next time."

"So much is riding on this, Matt," Adrian said. "If they close this department I'll be fine, and it'll be a real windfall for some team in India, but you and your whole team will be out on the street. Do you really want to risk that?"

"I know I can do it," Matt said, looking Adrian in the eye. He did his best to convey – with his tone of voice and body language – far more confidence than he actually felt in that moment. "I'm already working on improving these skills. The whole thing's a work-in-progress. In fact, um . . ." *was he really going to say this to Adrian?* ". . . I'm going to that Kyra Radcliffe workshop on presentation skills later this week. That will help a lot."

Adrian raised his eyebrows. "Kyra Radcliffe! She's in Cambridge?"

"Yes," Matt said, relaxing a bit. "She's doing a workshop called Creating Confidence for Presentations and I'm already signed up. It's a shame I couldn't take it before this meeting, but I'll have some solid skills to work with before the presentation next week."

The glance Adrian gave Matt seemed to be filled with a new level of respect. "You are taking this seriously, then?"

"Oh, absolutely!" Matt assured him. "I'm confident that with better preparation, I'll be able to succeed next time."

Fake it till you make it, he told himself again. It was becoming his mantra. He needed Adrian to give him a second chance and if that meant pretending to be more confident than he really felt, he was willing to do that.

91

It was much harder to fake that confidence when he got back to the office and saw the team waiting eagerly for the results.

"So what happened?" Amy asked, smiling hopefully. Justin and Steve were at her desk with cups of coffee in their hands. Clearly, everyone had been waiting for the news.

"We may not get it," he said, wincing a little at the disappointment in their eyes. "I wasn't expecting it, but they had a few of our competitors giving presentations too. The competition was stiff."

A little voice in his head had a much more negative opinion. If Matt had let that voice speak, it would've told the team: *I blew it! I completely screwed up. Probably, I should never have taken this job. I'm completely out of my depth here and have no idea what I'm doing. I'm self-absorbed and utterly clueless. Even though I genuinely did my best, it bombed . . . which means I'm a loser. Sad for me, but really bad news for you, because your jobs are riding on my ability to succeed!*

"But the data!" Justin said. "How could they not have been persuaded by that?"

Matt shrugged. A part of him wanted to treat them like friends and blurt out exactly what had happened, but he held himself back. They weren't his friends, they were his team. He needed to keep a certain distance, maintain his authority and try to hold onto their respect for as long as he could – even if it meant not admitting that he'd blown the presentation. The outcome was so personal for all of them. If they lost confidence in him now – or, worse, started to panic – it might influence their ability to help him prepare for the *second* presentation. And he really needed that one to go well! They all did.

Watching their shoulders sag as they went back to their desks, Matt felt real empathy for them. He'd gone into this presentation aware that all of their jobs were on the line. How could he not? Adrian rarely let him forget it! But seeing how downhearted they were about this failure made him really feel for them for the first time.

Before the guilt started weighing on him, he dashed off a text message to Vicki.

> Disastrous meeting!
> The presentation stank!
> ~ Matt

Within a few moments, Vicki text back, asking what had happened and offering encouragement. Matt realised that what he really wanted to do was talk to her on the phone.

> Need a friend. Can we Skype?
> ~ Matt
> Of course!
> ~ Vicki

Once they were talking, Vicki asked him to go through the situation, blow-by-blow. He was glad to hear how kind and sympathetic she was. And, even better, she seemed to perceive things he would never have noticed on his own. Instead of seeing the experience as a complete failure, he began to become aware of positive things about it, thanks to Vicki's point of view.

> **Our greatest glory consists not in never falling, but in rising every time we fall.** ~ *Confucius*

"Sounds like it's all about thinking about other people," Vicki said. Vicki couldn't help but find this an attractive quality in Matt. He'd always seemed like fun and had been easy to talk to, but lately, he'd been growing and changing in really appealing ways. She was impressed that he was willing to work so hard to make improvements.

"That's true," Matt said. "Adrian said I should pay more attention to what they wanted to hear and what questions they might have."

"You're also thinking about your team more, too," Vicki said. "Now their feelings and concerns are a lot more important to you. It's really motivating, isn't it?"

Now that she'd mentioned it, Matt did notice a shift taking place. All of the events of the morning seemed to be conspiring to get him to look outside himself and consider other people's wants and needs. He'd always thought of himself as pretty self-focused, so it didn't surprise him to be asked to consider others. But what Vicki said was surprising. It was much more motivating to take other people's concerns into consideration. It gave him a greater sense of responsibility and satisfaction.

"Do you ever hang out together after work?" Vicki asked.

"What? What do you mean?"

"Oh, you know, go across to the pub for some beer and a curry, that kind of thing."

Matt was stunned. He tried to picture it. Going out with the team seemed . . . well, unusual, but – now that she mentioned it – not a bad idea at all! "No, we never have," he told her. "But we could. Is that the kind of thing you do at work?"

"Absolutely," Vicki said. "It's a great way to build rapport and get to know your team."

"Isn't it too friendly? I'm trying to keep the line between management and staff pretty clear."

"You can do it without blurring any professional lines," Vicki told him. "Give it a try!"

"That's a great idea, Vicki. Thanks for taking the time to talk. It feels like you're right next door."

"Well, actually," Vicki swallowed hard before she said it. "I am coming to London soon to see my family. It's my brother's thirtieth birthday and he's having a big party. So I'll be in your neck of the woods."

"Fantastic," Matt said. "I didn't know if you ever came over here."

Vicki waited for him to say that they should get together, but he didn't. There was just an awkward pause.

"Well, I'd better get back to work," Matt said. "Thanks again for listening!"

"No problem," Vicki said. She hung up, confused. With the frequency and friendliness of their calls lately she was sure he would want to meet her. The moment she'd heard about her brother's party, meeting Matt was the first thing she'd thought of. But now, would she be coming to town without seeing him? Maybe she'd misunderstood what was going on between them. She couldn't help but feel disappointed.

Unaware of Vicki's expectations, Matt hung up feeling buoyant. When they had first started chatting, Matt hadn't really expected Vicki to become such an important part of his life. Now, it seemed, he was turning to her first – and getting more out of his conversations with her than with anyone else! She was really starting to matter to him. It gave him a warm feeling inside that he wasn't used to having.

This time, she'd even given him a quote that he was going to keep on his computer screen. She didn't know who had said it, but it fitted his situation perfectly:

> *Remember: you're not a failure if you don't make it. You're a success because you tried!*

Lessons

James wasn't in his office when Matt got back from the presentation. It was probably a good thing. Matt wanted to pull himself together and think of a professional way to present this fiasco to his mentor. It was not going to look good at his three-month review either, which was looming. Matt felt an urgent need to regroup and come up with a new game plan. How could things have gone so wrong?

When James returned to the office, he had already heard about the presentation from Adrian. Matt could only imagine the negative spin Adrian would have given it. He was dreading James's disappointment. But when their eyes met, what Matt saw was not blame or disappointment, but compassion and support. It was like the clouds clearing from the sky.

"So that didn't go as well as you'd hoped, did it?" James said, matter-of-factly, as he held the door open for Matt.

Matt walked past him quickly, with a deep sigh, and sat down across from James's desk. "No, it didn't." He was reluctant to look at James at first, imagining there would be accusations and stern advice to follow. He hoped James wouldn't go down the 'I'm so disappointed in you' route. Matt was willing to take the reprimand he had coming, but he'd always found the guilt-trip strategy very hard to take.

"When I was new to management," James said, "I thought I had to be right all the time. Somehow, I assumed that the people who had made it to the top got there without ever making a mistake."

Matt could barely believe it, James was actually smiling.

"Failure sucks," James said. "But failure is far more conducive to learning than success. You can really make it work for you. In fact, it's so effective at stimulating growth, that I've completely changed my mind about the people who make it to the top. Now, I believe that they're the ones who have used what they learned from failure to boost them up to the next level more quickly. The people who have one steady success after another without any disasters are very cautious. They don't take risks. They can succeed, slowly, but you're unlikely to see anything really astonishing from them, because astonishing success can only emerge when there's a lot at stake and risks are taken."

"So you're saying it's good to fail?" Matt asked, dumbfounded.

"Sometimes you need to look at things differently. Not as failures, but as results you didn't want, or weren't expecting. Do you know the story of the Post-It® note?" James asked. "It's one of the most successful office products ever invented, but it came from an embarrassing failure."

Matt thought about the Post-It® notes that littered his desk. He could hardly imagine keeping track of things without them.

"In 1970, a scientist named Spencer Silver, working at the 3M research laboratories, was asked to develop a super-strong adhesive. After elaborate tests, Silver did create a new adhesive, but it was hopelessly weak. No matter what Silver stuck it to, it could easily be lifted off. At 3M it was considered a total failure.

"Silver kept the formula, but couldn't imagine a use for it until Arthur Fry, another 3M scientist, realised he could use the weak adhesive to temporarily stick page markers into his hymnal at church without damaging the book itself. When 3M began distributing Post-it® notes in 1980, it soon became a legendary story of turning failure into success. It's a good reminder to always let your failures drive you towards success."

- *You're not a failure if you don't make it. You're a success because you try!*
- *Consider the impact on your team, not just yourself.*
- *Look at the people you are presenting to and be prepared to make adjustments according to their body language.*
- *Ask if there are questions. Don't expect others to tell you they don't understand.*
- *The understanding gained through discussion is more important than presenting data.*
- *Plan presentations thinking about the information from the audience's point of view.*
- *Spending social time with the team is a great way to build rapport and bond with them.*

Chapter 7

Kyra Radcliffe's Workshop

Matt rushed to Kyra Radcliffe's workshop as soon as he left work. He'd never been so eager to go to a workshop in his life. Whatever she told him had to work. The stakes were high. It was so important, he decided to do something completely unprecedented for him in a situation like this: take notes!

Learning to breathe

The first thing he wrote was a heading at the top of the page: **The Importance of Breathing.** When he read the words, the irony struck him. Breathing is important. What could be more obvious than that! Had he really paid money for this? He glanced around at the others in the workshop. Surely, no-one was buying this.

To his surprise, the others seemed to be taking notes and listening attentively. The idea of "learning to breathe" – something they'd all been doing successfully for years – apparently didn't strike them as ludicrous.

"Take slow, deep breaths," Kyra told the attentive crowd. "When we feel stressed, our breathing becomes shallow and fast. We tend to breathe from the upper part of the chest." She demonstrated breathing with the upper part of the lungs. Her shoulders rose and fell a little with each breath. "The top part of our lungs has less room to expand, so our lungs get less oxygen. This means that there is less oxygen reaching your brain, so you think less clearly and your heart has to beat faster to pump the oxygen around your body.

"Breathe deeply, instead!" she said, inhaling deeply. Most of the people in the room joined with her. Even Matt found himself automatically breathing more slowly and deeply. He had to admit, it was soothing. Maybe if he'd taken three deep breaths before that presentation – or during it! – he would have slowed down a bit and had time to notice the reactions of the other people in the room.

> **Tips for Confidence**
> - Breathe slowly and deeply.
> - Take a second to collect yourself.
> - Take three deep breaths when you're feeling stressed.

Coping with fear

"We all know what it's like to be afraid in a new situation," Kyra said. "All of us feel an element of fear when we're doing something unknown – whether we're going to meet someone new, setting up in business for the first time or travelling to a new city. We expect a certain amount of fear in challenging situations, but sometimes fear can crop up when we least expect it."

Matt knew exactly what she was talking about. He'd been nervous about the presentation to Millcreek, because he wanted to do it well, but it wasn't until they told him he had very little time that Matt had felt a twinge of fear. He'd never felt frightened in his previous position. Management was proving to be challenging every step of the way.

"Once you feel daunted by a project," Kyra continued, "you may start to ask yourself, 'Why did I put my name forward for this project?' If you allow negative self-talk into your mind, fear kicks in shortly afterwards. It's not the fear itself that is the problem – it's how you react to it that makes the difference."

A tall, professional-looking woman in the audience raised her hand. When Kyra acknowledged her, she stood by her chair. Matt couldn't read her name badge from where he was sitting, but he'd seen her come in with a group of bankers. "Last summer, I went to a seminar where they told us that fear was just imaginary, so we should ignore it, because it isn't real. It's all in our minds! Do you agree with that?"

Kyra smiled and moved closer to the audience. "It's all very well to rationalise the situation and tell yourself the fear is all in your mind, but whether it is in your mind or not, it is very real! Whether it's imaginary or justifiable makes no difference. The question is, how can you deal with it?"

"That's the important thing. How *can* you deal with it?" the woman asked, sitting back down with her group.

"There are many different ways," Kyra said. "Not all of them will work for you, but one of them will. The key is to give them all a go and find out which one or ones work for you in any given situation. The danger is that if an unexpected fear creeps up on you, you won't know what to do and you'll be paralysed by it. When that happens, you don't think straight. Logic goes straight out of the window and you're simply not at your best.

"The best way to avoid this situation is to find a strategy that works for you and practise it daily. That way, the next time you are confronted with fear, you'll already be skilled at putting your best strategy into use.

"A lot of the time we are afraid of doing it wrong or making a mistake. If you went into *any situation* knowing that the stakes were so high you could not afford to make a mistake, it would be terrifying. It would be like walking along the edge of a high-rise building, where the slightest misstep could send you hurtling over the edge to your death. Very few of our fears are based on that kind of danger. And yet, sometimes, we're so afraid of making a mistake that we feel as if they are!

"Allowing yourself to make mistakes is a crucial step to learning *anything* new. Just because we have left school doesn't mean we know everything and can stop learning now. Can you think back to a time when you didn't have a mobile phone? Do you remember wondering if you were doing it right when you tried to send your first text message? What about learning how to use predictive texting or sending emails? Technology is constantly changing, so we all learn new things all the time. Yet, sadly, I still hear people saying, 'I can't learn anything new' or 'I'm too old to change.' Is it true – or is that just another fearful, negative thought?"

Matt leaned forward, listening intently. He really wanted to understand this.

"Whenever you feel afraid of facing something new," Kyra said, "ask yourself what you're truly afraid of. If you're making a presentation and there's a lot on the line, you can think of it as fear of failure or fear of making a mistake. 'Failure' sounds huge. None of us wants to fail in life. But 'a mistake' sounds more forgivable, doesn't it? When you acknowledge that you're worried about making a mistake, it's far more manageable.

"Start there. Then try these strategies for coping with fear and see which ones work best for you."

This valuable information about coping with fear was worth the price of entry to Matt. He carefully copied down the steps on Kyra's PowerPoint projection, making notes of his own along the way. He wrote:

Strategies for Coping with FEAR

1. Deny it exists
Denial is an option. You can choose not to recognise any form of fear and pretend you don't have it. That means faking a confident persona and going for it – no matter how you feel.

2. Ignore it and get busy
Keeping yourself busy with work and other displacement activities can help you ignore your fear. It can work quite well as a short-term fix, but in the long term, it is likely to be unhealthy and unsustainable. We all know that workaholics are prone to come down with serious (sometimes fatal) stress-related illnesses. Befriending your fear is a better solution!

3. Befriend it
Fear is really your friend. You're not likely to push yourself out of your comfort zone without it. Fear tells you that

you're stretching your boundaries and creating new potential. The reason you are fearful is that you are growing! Don't let yourself hesitate and get stuck in negative thinking. Step up and greet fear as you would an old friend. Welcome it and continue to do whatever you fear.

Next, a graphic showing a flow of energy appeared on the screen, as Kyra explained, "Our energy flows throughout our bodies and keeps us alive. This flow is dependent on our positive, supportive thoughts. Negative thoughts stop the energy flowing.

"This effect is clearly demonstrated using a stress-relief technique from kinesiology (also known as 'muscle testing' or 'energy testing'). A kinesiologist will tell you that our thoughts, beliefs, emotions and attitudes are connected with energy points on the body (also known as 'energy meridians'). These meridians are energy channels for the body. Each of them supports specific muscles and organs. Kinesiology links elements of traditional Chinese medicine – such as acupuncture, meridians and energy balancing – with Western muscle testing and physiology. Its purpose is to bring about balance in the body by releasing energy blocks.

"If, for example, you have a stressful thought, belief or attitude, a strong muscle will weaken when tested. Negative thoughts block the free flow of energy to that muscle. When you replace that negative thought with a positive thought, the muscle will immediately regain its integrity and be strong again. Similarly, muscle testing can reveal imbalances in the body which are related to nutrition, learning difficulties, dyslexia, pain, injuries and other problems.

"Just one thought can affect us – whether it's positive or negative. A positive thought will support the energy in our bodies and keep it flowing. A negative thought will stop the energy flow in its tracks."

"What happens to the energy when it's blocked?" the woman at the back asked.

"Imagine the energy flow is like a stream with a tight bend," Kyra said. "When you have a positive thought, it adds a bit more water to the stream. The flow is either continuous or it gets even stronger, depending on the amount of positive water that is added. If the thought is a negative one, it is like adding twigs to the stream. Only a few twigs are necessary to get caught up in the bend and cause a blockage. Little negative thoughts, chattering in the back of your mind are enough to do it. 'I can't believe I said that to him', 'I'll never be any good at this', 'I don't know why I try, it's hopeless'. They take only seconds to think, but they can block the flow of energy for moments, or, if they pile up together, they can reroute the stream entirely! One big negative thought can be like adding a whole tree trunk at once and – wham! – the stream is blocked. And no-one wants that. Every organ, every part of your body needs a healthy flow of energy at all times. Otherwise, problems develop and can become severe."

Matt shifted in his chair. The idea of blockages in his body made him uneasy. He stretched his legs out in front of him to ease his circulation, before looking at Kyra again. He suddenly realised he'd been listening for quite a while now without doubting the information she was giving them. He was really taking it all in. Who would've expected it? If only Vicki could see him now.

"Let me give you an example," Kyra was saying. "If you press on your index finger and cut off the blood circulation for a moment, your finger will turn red, then blue. It's not very dangerous. When you release the pressure, it quickly returns to normal. But if you tie a band tightly around it – in that same spot – and leave it there, you will lose your finger because of it! That is the difference between a momentary negative thought and a chronic habit of negativity that can block your energy and lead to all kinds of problems. What happens then? If there are no positive thoughts to help counteract the negative ones it can cause a distinct lack of energy, and even illness.

"It's worth your effort to get rid of negative thoughts."

> **A positive attitude may not solve all your problems, but it will annoy enough people to make it worth the effort.** ~ *Herm Albright*

Eliminating negative thoughts

Kyra went on to say that many of us feed ourselves a constant stream of negative thoughts. They cause our bodies to release those toxic chemicals into our system that Matt had read about on the website. These chemicals increase our physical, as well as our emotional, stress levels.

"A lot of people disparage positive thinking as being unrealistic,"

Kyra admitted. "They assume that looking at negative possibilities is an important part of 'seeing things as they really are'. But the truth is, just because you can see the good in a bad situation, it does not necessarily mean that you are avoiding the truth. I'm certainly not advocating that you look at the weeds in your garden and say, 'there are no weeds' and then expect the weeds to die without taking any action yourself.

"But because of the way your brain responds to positive thinking, there's every reason to use positive thoughts like weed killer! If your body is going to release chemicals that boost your confidence and thereby improve your chances for success – every time you think a positive thought – why not use it to your advantage?"

Matt had never thought of positive thinking like this before. Most of the people in the room had been born long after Dale Carnegie started promoting "positive thinking" in the middle of the twentieth century. So it had become a tired cliché. If Kyra was right, it was decades later before scientists had begun to understand the relationships between beneficial chemicals like endorphins, and positive thinking. The connection between body posture and positive thinking was an even more recent discovery.

"It's very hard to think a positive thought if you've got that negative physiology going on," Kyra said. "You can make it much easier to think positively and stay in a positive frame of mind if you position your body in a positive posture. Keep your back straight, your head up and your chin up. Then put a smile on your face. When you do that, you have literally created a happy home for your thoughts and released the endorphins. Let's all try it now!

Chin up. Shoulders back. Hold your head a little higher . . . now . . . smile."

Matt felt a little self-conscious about it, but when he glanced around the room, he saw everyone else joining in, so he didn't feel quite as uneasy. He squared his shoulders and changed the position of his head and chin. As soon as he did, he realised that this was a posture he almost never maintained in the course of a day. If this was "positive physiology" he certainly wasn't making use of it.

Slowly, he added a smile to top it off. It was easy enough to do with everyone in the room, including Kyra, smiling at each other. Amazingly enough, the mood of the entire room had lifted in a matter of seconds. The audience had changed from a group of quiet, sombre listeners to happy, active participants – just by changing their body posture. It was remarkable.

"Body posture is not just something that would make your mother happy!" Kyra laughed. "It's a very powerful tool for generating the kind of body chemistry that will make you feel powerful, strong and confident every day."

Next to Matt, a man named Wilson, from a leading IT company in Cambridge, raised his hand. "I heard a story, but don't know if it's true, that Milton Erickson, the father of hypnotherapy, used posture to help people with depression. When someone came to see him, he told him, 'I'll be busy for a few minutes. In the meantime, why don't you go outside for ten minutes and count the number of chimney pots you see.' That client walked down the street, tilting his head up for ten minutes and immediately felt better. By the time he got back, he was so cheered up, he didn't need treatment."

"That's a great story," Kyra said. "It's a perfect example of the kinds of strategies you can use to get your physiology working for you.

"If you're walking down the street and you're feeling miserable, you tend to look at your feet or the cracks in the paving. Without knowing it, you're asking your body to keep you feeling miserable. Your head is down and your emotions will stay down as well. If you look up or make eye contact with other people, it changes the chemicals in your brain, which changes the way that you feel. So if you're feeling low, one strategy for changing your mood is to assume 'things are looking up' and act accordingly."

Things Are Looking Up

Take a walk down the street. Instead of staring at the pavement or things around you at eye level, look up! See what the shop windows on the top floors are like. Look for chimney pots and flag poles. How many weather vanes can you see?

If you've never spent time looking toward the tops of buildings, you might be surprised by what you've been missing. Just ten minutes noticing things that are higher than your normal eye level can do wonders.

"Another thing you might try, while you're looking at the chimney pots," Kyra continued, "is to smile at the people you pass as you stroll along. Have you ever walked down a street and looked at the other people – I mean, *really looked*? Have you taken the time to wonder about their lives, their hopes and dreams? People-watching is a fascinating occupation and much of what we make up about other people is based purely on what we can see. How kempt do they look? What do you think they eat? Do you think they smoke or work out – or both?

"With even the quickest glance, you can form opinions about the healthiness of their lifestyles. From the way they walk, you might make an assessment of what they think about themselves. Does their walk show they are feeling confident? Is their head held high? Do they look you in the eye as they pass or – even more rare these days – do they smile at you in return?

"When you see an old man with hunched shoulders and an unshaven face shuffling along with his eyes downcast, you don't assume that he was once a smart city-slicker, do you? You may be wrong. Yet, the thing is, we make our judgements based on what we see now – not on people's pasts. A lady clicking high heels firmly on the pavement, with a carefully made-up face, well-groomed hair and a smart coat over her clothes conveys a sense of importance and worth. You might start to feel she is someone of significance when you see her. At least she thinks she is! And she's presenting herself to the world in a way that supports her opinion and non-verbally persuades others to draw the same conclusion.

"So how do you look to others on the street? What level of confidence are you conveying? How is your opinion of yourself coming through? Do you persuade others that you are important and significant by your posture and the way you dress? Or are you revealing your fear, anxiety and doubt?"

Matt thought back to the outfit he had worn at Millcreek. Brigit had spent so much time helping him get it right. It was meant to convey confidence in the way he dressed, at least (even if it was actually a sign of his confidence that Brigit knew what she was doing!), but what had his posture been like? Did he smile at them enough? He had smiled and shaken their hands firmly when they arrived, but not during the presentation.

He winced to remember how he'd literally kept his back to them the whole time. How could he have been so careless! He'd let his anxiety about the time crunch take over and dampen the effect of everything else.

Now that he thought about it, Matt realised he'd spent a lot of time indulging in negative thoughts that day as well – from the moment he'd decided Adrian was hoping he'd fail to the moment he'd had to face his team and tell them he'd failed. *Well, it may be a negative thought*, Matt told himself, *but it's the truth. I did fail. No way around that. If I think about what happened at all, it's negative: a failure.* Despite the good, supportive things Vicki had said, Matt had let himself believe the worst about the situation.

Lessons

Matt had never taken so many notes in his life. Even in school, he was never a big note taker. In this situation, he had a completely different level of motivation. Instead of being concerned with the immediate future – his grades or a short-term performance – Matt was determined to permanently improve his skills. For the first time in his life, he was approaching these lessons with long-term considerations in mind. He wanted to master these skills so he could build a life of confidence and success.

In the beginning, he had been taking notes so he'd have something to discuss with James. Then he'd realised they would also be useful for his three-month review. Now, he was taking them for himself. He'd come to realise that this information had real personal value for him – apart from the interests of his job or even his mentor.

Matt wanted to be the kind of confident, secure person Kyra was describing. He could see how it would help him in every area of his life. Instead of just jotting down notes automatically every time Kyra made a list, Matt began to think more carefully about what she was saying and ask himself what *he* needed to know, what *he* wanted to incorporate into his life. It changed the way he was taking notes, but it also changed the way he was reinforcing these points in his mind. Suddenly, it was as if he were saying, *"Remember this! It's important"* every time he wrote something down.

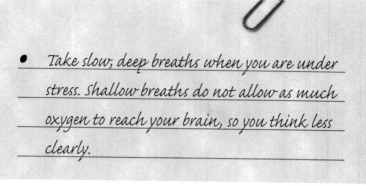

- Take slow, deep breaths when you are under stress. Shallow breaths do not allow as much oxygen to reach your brain, so you think less clearly.

- There is almost always time to take a few seconds to collect yourself.
- Find a strategy you like for coping with fear and practise it daily, so you'll be ready to use it the next time you need it.
- Allow yourself to make mistakes. It is a crucial step in learning.
- Befriend your fear. It tells you that you are growing and stepping outside your comfort zone.
- Beware of little negative thoughts chattering in the back of your mind. Over time, they can drain your energy and even make you physically ill.
- Seeing good in a bad situation does not necessarily mean you are avoiding the truth.
- Our brains are designed to release the most productive chemicals when we think positive thoughts. Why not take advantage of that fact? It's easy to do. Just think positively!

Chapter 8

Learning to Think Positively

Kyra's Story

"Now, some of you are going to think this is a silly story, at first," Kyra began. "It's not from the workplace, it's from childhood. But once you hear it, I think you'll see how well it applies. Bear with me . . ."

Two Left Feet

For most of my early life, I lived with the assumption that I couldn't dance. A few incidents persuaded me that I was not a dancer and, until I challenged those assumptions, I never doubted it. For some, it's maths or spelling, for me, it was dancing.

It all started when I was eight years old and my family moved house. Every May at my new school, there was a village fete. As part of the celebration, all the children were meant to participate in a May Day Dance. As preparation, we were taught country dancing.

During one of the early lessons, I messed up the steps – not once, not twice, but three times. On seeing it, my dance teacher said, "Kyra Radcliffe, you have two left feet!"

That hurt. Even though I was trying very hard and eventually learned the dance, I came away from the experience believing that I couldn't dance. My teacher had

117

said so, in so many words, and I believed her without questioning it.

In secondary school, teenage discos turned my social life into a nightmare. Since all my friends hung out at the disco I had to go, but whenever I could, I played table tennis or pool in the corner, while the rest of my friends were on the dance floor. They seemed to be enjoying themselves with effortless ease, but I knew that wouldn't happen for me – because I had two left feet: I couldn't dance. For one school party, we went to a joint disco with a local grammar school. Unfamiliar surroundings only made it worse. I found their dance floor very imposing. Even though I wanted desperately to be liked by the boys, I felt I had no hope of succeeding in this environment.

And then, just as I was feeling my least self-confident, my best friend pulled me out onto the dance floor! I was mortified. There I stood in the middle of the floor, with all the grace of an elephant doing pirouettes. Everyone was looking at me. So, even though I'd managed to avoid it for years, I danced. With no experience to speak of, I had no idea how to move. Being tense and nervous is not conducive to dancing either. I made a mess of it. For some reason that eludes me completely now, I kept my hands clenched, with my elbows by my side, and tried to sway my body in sync with the music. If I'd been trying to do an impression of someone dancing awkwardly, I couldn't have done better.

Not surprisingly, my friend teased me for acting like a boxer on the dance floor. Repeating the horrible, negative message that had been on a feedback loop in my head since I was eight, I said, "I've got two left feet."

So that was it. My "I can't dance" belief was well and truly confirmed. There was no question now. I knew it and everyone else did too – not just in my school, but in the whole town! "Kyra can't dance. She's like a boxer with two left feet, an elephant attempting pirouettes. It's pitiful."

It wasn't until my late twenties that I was persuaded, with great reluctance, to go to ballroom dancing lessons with some friends, because they needed an extra lady to balance the numbers. I knew I couldn't dance and I didn't want to go, but I agreed to go "just once".

As the teacher described the steps, I paid careful attention. Then she turned the music on and let us try the moves ourselves, with a partner. Since I knew what the moves were, I didn't completely humiliate myself. In fact, I was astonished to find I didn't trip over my feet once!

"You've got a good sense of rhythm," my partner told me.

After twenty years believing I couldn't dance, I felt really flattered. Later that evening, I felt even better, when I found out that he had danced with the Cambridge University Ballroom Dancing team. What esteemed company!

In the weeks that followed, I eagerly went back for more lessons. With further encouragement, I gradually learned how to dance. After so many years of negative assumptions, my success was especially sweet. But the benefits went even further than that. I found that not only could I dance, I loved to dance!

By now I have learned not only ballroom, but Latin, modern jive, rock & roll and salsa. Not bad for someone with two left feet!

> **Good timber does not grow with ease;**
> **the stronger the wind the stronger the trees.**
> ~ *J. Willard Marriott*

Listen to your thoughts

"As adults we place high expectations on ourselves and abhor failure. We want things to be right and to be perfect the first time around. And we hang on to beliefs we gained in our childhood that may no longer be true – whether or not we have any current supporting evidence. Why not give ourselves a break?

"You are with yourself all the time. But have you ever really spent time listening to yourself? If you did, what would you hear?" Kyra asked. "Would the voice inside your head tell you that you are a great person, generous, loving and supportive? Or would it say that you are no good because you didn't get the report done on time, or you raised your voice to the children when they came home, or you hit the kerb when you parked the car?

"Most of us, if we are honest, don't listen to our own thoughts enough to critique the critic. Instead when our internal voice starts criticising something we've done or failed to do, we automatically go, 'Oh, OK. Yeah, that was bad . . . embarrassing . . . I can't believe I did that.' We swallow it whole and accept the underlying belief without question.

"Start paying attention to what you are saying to yourself. What's going on in your head from the moment you wake up to the time you go to bed? Once you begin to monitor your thoughts, the next step is to intervene. Instead of just accepting whatever you hear, challenge it! Where did that idea come from? Is it based on something someone else told you? How valid is it? Is it simply an expression of a feeling of anxiety or low self-esteem or is there any evidence to support it? If someone else said such a thing to you, what would you say to argue against it?

"Negative thoughts can sneak up on you," Kyra continued. "If you let yourself start thinking they're justified, it's much harder to shake them loose. But there's one way that most people find works exceptionally well.

"Think about your best friend. When you're feeling low, what things do they say to you? Do they offer you encouragement and support? Or do they tear you down and make you feel worse about yourself? If they did that, they wouldn't be your friend for long, would they?

"Whenever you have trouble eliminating negative thoughts, ask yourself this: would I put up with this from a friend? The answer may surprise you. Often we get so used to the negative comments inside our own heads that we don't even notice how completely unacceptable and mean-spirited they are! If someone else spoke to us in this way, we would know they were toxic and immediately get away from them. Why should we put up with this kind of toxic thinking anywhere – even in the privacy of our own thoughts?"

Thinking back on the meeting with Millcreek, Matt remembered some of the things he'd told himself. If a friend had told him he was self-absorbed and an utterly clueless loser, he'd be highly offended. Why should he allow himself to be insulted by anyone – even by his own mind!

An accountant in the audience was sharing his own version of negative thinking. "I used to sit at my desk, hour after hour, with this little voice muttering in the back of my head, criticising me all day long. I was so used to it, I didn't even hear it any more!"

"Your body heard it, though," Kyra said. "It was dumping stressful chemicals into your bloodstream all day."

"It's true," the man agreed. "I'd come home at night with these pounding headaches and I couldn't understand why. When I read about negative thinking in your book, at first I actually thought that I never did that!" Several people laughed and nodded, as if they'd been there before too. "But then I realised I did it all the time. It was like a constant drone. No wonder my head hurt!"

"What kind of things were you thinking?"

"When I finally started listening to it, I realised it was like having a cranky little old man following me around all day, saying, 'That's not right. Don't do that. Do it this way.' Constantly second-guessing and criticising everything I did!"

"And would you ever dream of letting anyone else talk to you that way?" Kyra asked.

"Never!" the accountant said. "If anyone followed me around saying negative things like that, I'd go to great lengths to avoid them. I would never let an employer talk to me like that, much less a friend."

I am Going to be a Millionaire

Another strategy for creating confidence is to make a powerfully confident statement.

"I am feeling confident" doesn't help you at all, because it isn't true and you know it. If you felt confident, you wouldn't be trying out a strategy that is meant to create confidence. (And you're not that easy to fool!) Affirmations like this are worthless because they contradict what you already know is going on inside your own head.

But if you say, "I am growing more confident every day" it is powerful, positive – and has the advantage of actually being a true statement. You can believe it. It is much more effective. And it has action.

What you have done is create a *gestalt* between your current reality and the reality you are creating inside your head. Your brain is galvanised into action to do something about the statements that you've made. If you keep your positive thoughts going, then your subconscious mind will be looking for any way possible for you to achieve those goals.

So, if you're thinking of becoming a millionaire, your mind will look for ways in which you can create your millions. Don't bother trying to put one over on yourself by saying, "I am a millionaire". (There may be "a sucker born every minute", but it isn't you. Or if it is, you'll soon be brought back to reality the moment you go out and try to spend your millions!)

So whatever you tell yourself, make sure it's something you can put the full force of your belief behind. "I'm getting richer every day" may be a stretch. "I'm destined to become a millionaire" might work, if you like that fateful sort of tone. "I'm becoming a millionaire" will almost certainly sound persuasive . . . if it's millions you are after!

Life does not always comply with our wishes, but confidence is 100 percent reliant on what kind of thoughts we think. It's up to you to reinforce the positive thoughts that make you feel confident and eliminate the negative thoughts that fill you with uncertainty and doubt. Unlike so many things, this is something over which you have complete control. Take advantage of it!

"The human brain is a fascinating piece of equipment," Kyra continued. "Some people have likened it to a computer, which is true in some ways. Computer programmers have a saying:

garbage in, garbage out. Our brains are certainly similar in that way!

"If you tell your brain one thing, then contradict it with another, your brain won't argue. It will go with whatever you tell it and believe that to be true. If you keep repeating something over and over, like 'I always blow my presentations' or 'I'm no good at this', your brain will assume you're right. It's very accommodating in that way.

"As I said earlier, our energy flows throughout our bodies and this flow is dependent on our supportive thoughts. Why do I say that? Because negative thoughts stop the flow of energy! Just one thought can affect the flow. A positive thought gives support to the energy and keeps it flowing, a negative thought stops the energy flow in its tracks.

"When you start to feel negative, your confidence is the first thing to go. We associate confidence with vigour, because confidence often goes hand-in-hand with positive energy. Negative, doubting, self-destructive energy quite naturally works to undermine your confidence.

"We used to believe our thoughts were ethereal. With today's technology, we finally understand enough about how the brain works to recognise that thoughts directly impact the flow of energy in our bodies!

"For a thought to exist, it requires a pulse to move from one neuron to another. The message jumps across the synaptic gap to be received by that next neuron's dendrites and you think. The old saying, 'You are what you think' can now be verified by the activity in the brain.

"And it goes even further. It's not just the firing of neurons that affects us, but our energy fields as a whole. The vibrations of these fields are in sync with our thoughts. If we have negative thoughts, they vibrate with that negative energy. We literally create a wave field around us that is negative and disruptive to our well-being – and that of others who come into contact with us.

"Have you ever felt someone enter the room and known immediately what mood they were in – even before they spoke and before you looked at them? You may have noticed that when some people come into a room, they bring happiness and enthusiasm with them. We often say that someone like this 'lights up a room' when they enter. Unfortunately, it can work the other way as well. There are people who skulk into a room dragging such a bad mood with them that everything goes a little darker when they come in. These people drain your energy with their negativity, don't they?

"The energy inside us is real. So it makes sense that it can have a very real effect on the world around us. When we maintain positive thoughts, we create a positive energy field which attracts harmonious, positive fields from others. This amplifies our positive thinking and allows our own energy to flow more freely through our bodies. Just imagine how much smoother and more pleasant our interactions with others would be if we were constantly emitting a positive, happy, confident field of energy!

"I'll take it a step further," Kyra smiled. "Think how much more powerful and well-received your presentations will be if you consciously maintain a positive energy field by emitting confident, optimistic thoughts!"

Time Limit on Negativity

If you can't fend off your negativity any other way, at least give yourself a time limit! Put a limitation on how long you're going to indulge your negative thoughts.

For instance, you might say to yourself, "For the next five minutes, I'm going to really let rip. Whatever hateful, negative, ridiculous, self-loathing, demoralising, completely over-the-top negative thing I want to say to myself, I'll permit it. But the clock is ticking. In five minutes flat, it's over. Then it's time for a return to sanity." (Ridiculing the very idea of negative thoughts never hurts either!)

Maybe you'd prefer to go to that dark, negative place for longer. You could make it thirty minutes or an hour or five hours, for that matter – if you really want to be that long. Some situations require more mulling and draw from a longer, more complicated history than others. So, inevitably, some will need more space. But not too much space. The important thing is that you assert control. Knowing you can have negative thoughts is fine. It makes you human. But it's vital that you are not at the mercy of negativity rampaging through your brain and undermining your life, your relationships and your success.

Your best friend

"When I asked you to think about your best friend, how many of you thought of someone other than yourself?" Kyra asked.

Everyone in the room, including Matt, raised their hand. Matt had thought first of Brigit and Brad, but Vicki had also come to mind. Whenever he thought of her, a pleasant feeling came over him. She was starting to become a part of his life.

"What qualities make this person your friend?"

"Kindness," the accountant said.

"Supportiveness," someone else said.

Others chimed in, adding qualities like love, generosity, honesty and good-heartedness.

"Think for a moment. Do you have these qualities yourself?" Kyra let her eyes roam around the room, watching people as they reflected on her question. "Sure, you may offer these qualities to others, but the sad thing is, the way we treat other people is not always the way we treat ourselves.

"Let me make a radical suggestion: what if you could be your own best friend? If your best friend has to be someone who is kind, supportive, loving, generous, honest and good-hearted, would you have to change the way you treat yourself to qualify?"

The room had become very quiet. Matt didn't know what everyone else was thinking, but he was feeling a little embarrassed. How many times had he turned to Brigit for support because he was coming down so hard on himself that he couldn't stand to listen to it any more? It was as if she were protecting him from his own negative thoughts! Pretty shocking, when he thought about it. If he was going to eliminate those negative thoughts and be his own best friend, it was going to take some real effort.

"What if you could support yourself through words?" Kyra said, pulling up a chair near the audience. "What if, instead of being your worst critic – picking up on every fine point of what went wrong, what you need to fix about yourself, how you looked to everyone else – you were your own most stalwart support? What if you could rely on yourself to acknowledge how you are feeling, show you care, put forward good suggestions, and, most of all, squash any attempts to criticise yourself?"

"I would love that," the woman from the bank said. "But how do you do it? This critical voice in my head seems to stay awake, nagging me, twenty-four hours a day."

"Why not start by doing what your external best friend does – listen to yourself! Take time to hear what you are saying. Are your thoughts supporting you or undermining you? Are they the kind of things your best friend would say or do they sound more like your worst critic?

"The brilliant thing is, you get to decide what you want to say to yourself. What would you like to hear? How can you be more supportive, a better listener, a better friend?

"The truth is, no external friend can say exactly what you want to hear all the time – but you can! If you let yourself, you can *always say the perfect thing*. Instead of wishing someone would say the thing you need to hear, you can say it. How perfect is that?

"From now on, start to talk to yourself as if you were your best friend. And one more thing . . ." Kyra paused, looking somewhat mischievous. "Do it aloud!!"

Some people groaned. Others giggled. Everyone seemed a bit uncomfortable with the idea. "The neighbours will think I'm mad!" someone said.

"That's your negative voice speaking," Kyra laughed. "No matter how silly it seems, one of the most powerful techniques I know for building up confidence is what I like to call: Talking to Yourself".

Talking to Yourself

1. Make an Appointment
Choose a particular time every day or every week that suits you to have a regular conversation with your best friend.

2. Find a Mirror
This technique works best if you're actually looking at yourself. The bathroom mirror will work fine. A hand-held mirror will suffice. If you're really brave, a full-length mirror is great.

3. Look Yourself in the Eye
Face yourself. Even if you can't exactly shake your own hand, you can look yourself in the eye and make contact.

4. Say What You Like About Yourself
Your best friend knows things about you that no-one else knows – good things and bad. You can trust a friend to remind you of your strengths and successes when you're feeling low. Do the same thing for yourself now. Compliment yourself on your good

qualities. Point out your strengths and talents. Remind yourself that you have a lot to offer – and be specific about what it is!

5. Acknowledge Yourself

Who knows better than you do what efforts you've put into things? Sometimes not even your external best friend knows how hard you've tried or what you've sacrificed or how much you've grown. But you do. Who's going to acknowledge it, if you don't? Praise yourself for the way you are managing the things you face. Acknowledge yourself for the efforts you put in – the times you have kept quiet and the times you've spoken out for yourself. Recognise the strides you've made. Let yourself know how proud you are of all your efforts.

6. Tell Yourself You Love You

End the conversation by telling yourself – your best friend – how much you love yourself. Hold eye contact with yourself for a few seconds to receive the love you are giving yourself. Then thank yourself for taking the time to have this conversation. Let yourself know you'll always be a support for yourself. Promise that, no matter what, you'll always be on your own side.

Lessons

Matt tried to picture himself smiling at his face in the mirror and saying, "I love you, darling!" Maybe if he were practising to tell a girl . . . but saying it to himself almost made him blush.

Kyra was suggesting things now that took him a long way from familiar territory. Matt had never even considered the possibility of paying attention to his thoughts! The idea of intervening in what was going on in his head was a completely new concept to him.

In the past, he'd always assumed that his thoughts were an indigenous part of his personality. If someone challenged his way of thinking, he'd say, "That's just who I am!" He'd heard his father and his uncles say this kind of thing as he was growing up. He still remembered one of his teachers saying, "People don't change". His father had said the same thing and Matt had never questioned it. When people said, "Don't expect people to change" the implication was that no-one would change – not Matt and not the person saying it. He'd accepted that as truth since the time he was about seven years old.

And yet, as soon as he heard Kyra describe the way to intervene in negative thoughts and stop them before they created a toxic chemical state in your body, Matt knew she was right. Of course that was possible! He'd simply never questioned those old messages he'd internalised as a child. Now he realised the most dynamic people he knew changed all the time. Even James had said he was not good at people skills when he first became a manager, but now they were an expertise he was widely known and respected for. James was right. If he could learn these skills, Matt could too.

- *Pay attention to your thoughts. What are you saying to yourself?*
- *If you hear a negative thought, challenge it! Is there any evidence for its accusation or is it an expression of fear or anxiety?*
- *If it's hard to stop a negative thought, ask if you'd put up with a remark like that from a friend?*
- *If all else fails, put a time limit on your negativity.*
- *Only use affirmations that sound true to you. ("I am feeling confident" is just a cheerful lie, if you don't feel confident. Why insult yourself with something obviously untrue? Try wording it in a way you can truly believe. "I am growing more confident every day " is better.)*

- *If you consciously maintain a positive energy field by emitting confident, optimistic thoughts, your presentations will be far more effective.*
- *Be your own best friend.*
- *Make an appointment to talk to yourself – positively! – on a regular basis.*

Chapter 9

Feeling Inspired

When Kyra began to talk about making a confident presentation, Matt listened very carefully. How he wished he'd known about some of these things before he went to Millcreek!

"Make sure your first impression is a confident one!" Kyra said. "You never get a second chance to make a first impression. So, what impression do you want to make?"

Matt tried to imagine what kind of first impression he might have made on Ramta, but nothing came to mind. In actuality, he hadn't been paying attention to the impression he was making when they met, he had been thinking about what he was going to say in the presentation later. So he had shaken Ramta's hand, looked her in the eye and completely forgotten about her. There was no way to be sure whether he'd made a good first impression or not, when he had no memory of Ramta's non-verbal reaction or body language at the time. He wondered if he'd seemed confident or just preoccupied and self-absorbed.

"Before meeting someone," Kyra continued, "Spend some time thinking about this: how will you speak? What will your body language be like? What will you wear? After all that preparation, don't let a last minute rush get the better of you! Take a split second to compose yourself before you knock on the door, enter the room, or walk over to the person you're meeting.

"A first meeting often starts with a handshake. Make sure your handshake lets the other person know that you are confident (regardless of how you are really feeling). Offer your hand and shake theirs with a firm – but not vice-like – grip for a couple of seconds. Meet their eyes and smile."

Tips for Confidence
- Take a split second to compose yourself.
- Offer your hand to shake.
- Make eye contact.
- Shake hands with a firm (not vice-like) grip.
- Keep smiling.

"The confidence that shows up in your body is often a reflection of your thoughts," Kyra explained. "If you control your thinking, by thinking the right thoughts, it will go a long way to giving you a more confident appearance. It's just as vital you give your brain good thoughts to mull on, as it is to give it good body signals.

"Believing you can do something and creating confidence is not about lying to yourself – it's about being realistic and keeping a positive frame of mind! Be the person you would like to be in your mind. Then stand back and watch as that feeling works its way through your body and into your actions!"

> **You are today where your thoughts have brought you; you will be tomorrow where your thoughts take you.** ~ *James Allen*

Matt liked the sound of this. He was starting to realise he did have a deep belief that he could be an excellent project manager. When he had told Adrian he would be able to do the second presentation well, he had been faking that confidence a little, but there was also a quiet voice inside him that said, "You're right! You *can* do a good job at this."

Kyra's idea about being who he wanted to be made sense to him. Maybe he could position himself in his mind to be the successful, effective presenter he could imagine himself being – and that would have a powerful effect on his performance.

All this time, he'd had little doubt in his ability to do his job. He'd always excelled at it, without giving much thought to how he was doing it or how it was affecting other people. But, after the fiasco at Millcreek, he could use all the help he could get! Why not use the power of his own mind to help him?

When he visualised what he wanted to happen at the next presentation, it looked so different from the first one. In his imagination, he was a skilled presenter, providing his potential clients with valuable information, always checking in with them to see what their needs were. (Did they understand what he'd said so far? Did they have any questions?) He imagined himself being really adept at explaining exactly what they could do for their clients and making them *want it!*

Now he could see why so many people raved about Kyra's training. When she emphasised that the mind is hugely powerful and explained that visualising things can have a big impact on performance, Matt completely believed her. He couldn't wait to try it out.

Building Confidence Brick-By-Brick

This exercise is called the 'Brick Wall Confidence Builder' because it lets you build your confidence one brick at a time.

1. Draw an outline of a brick wall on a piece of paper.
2. On each brick, write down something you have achieved.

It can be anything you're proud of doing in your life or any skills you have learned. "I learned to drive" is one example. Others might include: "I learned to speak French" or "I learned to use PhotoShop™".

Things related to your family can have bricks of their own: "I have a wonderful daughter (and/or son)" or "I sent my children through university" or "I married someone I love".

Don't forget occupational achievements: "I found an excellent job in my field" or "I won the award for best salesperson of the month".

Vocational and recreational activities count as well: "I arranged our delightful trip to Singapore" or "I have become a versatile gourmet cook".

Write down anything you know you're good at. It can be a small, daily thing, such as "I'm good at getting out of bed in the morning" or "I'm good at brushing my teeth" or "I'm good at driving".

It can involve social skills, for example: "I'm good at listening to people" or "I'm good at talking" or "I'm good at being a friend".

It can involve work skills, like: "I'm great at dealing with customers" or "I'm excellent at analysis" or "I'm great at making presentations".

When you run out, think about things you did well today and make bricks for each of them. This is your own wall. Also, write down all the achievements you have ever had in your life. Everything counts: passing your driving test, graduating from university, the birth of your children, getting your first job, moving into your first apartment. Give yourself credit for all of the accomplishments of your life. Isn't it time you acknowledged yourself for how much you've done and how far you've come?

3. Take one week to build your wall. Every day, keep thinking of new things you're good at and putting them on a brick.

It can be so hard to think of *anything* you're good at, or you have achieved, when you're feeling low or lacking in confidence. So jot as many of them down now as you can.

Take a small notebook round with you and fill up the pages with lists of things you have done well. Have fun with it! Start at the beginning: put down learning to walk! That's one of the biggest achievements each of us has. The average baby falls down many times before taking its first step. You may laugh at the idea of including this, but think about what it would be like if you'd never learned to walk! So, give yourself credit for it. Learning to drive is another good one. It's so inconvenient if you don't know how to do it that you should definitely be acknowledged for taking the initiative to learn to do it well. Any time you've passed an exam, it's worth noting too. And how about simple things, like smiling at a stranger and saying hello, having the courage to ask for what you want in a shop, or discussing your preference for where you'd like to go on a date. Make sure there is a mix of things that you do well. Include anything that you've received recognition from others for or would like to acknowledge yourself. Add these to your brick wall.

4. At the end of a week, take a look at your brick wall. It's pretty substantial, isn't it? Now, you can say to yourself, "Well, look, if I can do this many things . . ."

5. Ask yourself: how many of these bricks have I had negative thoughts about? It's easy to get into the habit of having negative thoughts about ourselves – even in relation to the things we're good at! What could be more ridiculous?

Think of your confidence as a solid, brick wall – not based on one or two things, but on every one of these bricks. Support yourself. Encourage yourself. These bricks represent things you're really good at. Give yourself credit for that! You deserve it.

"Before you go to bed tonight," Kyra said, "think about what's going to happen tomorrow. See it in a positive light – where things are working and going right. Imagine everything going just the way you want it, even if you really think it won't. You'll be amazed by the results!"

Matt imagined the next presentation going brilliantly and the client signing a long-term contract. If he was going to dream, he even imagined Millcreek miraculously calling back and giving him a second chance – even though he couldn't really believe that would happen. Why not visualise exactly what he *wanted* to happen?

Tips for Confidence

- Create your own confidence!
- Visualise what you want to happen.
- Spend time each day focusing on future events in a positive way.
- Imagine things going well.

Visualising the ideal situation and imagining himself to be the person he really wanted to be would certainly stop a lot of the negative thoughts in his head. Matt especially wanted to be rid of the ones telling him the weight of the whole department was on his shoulders and he was sure to be out on the street, looking for work, after these presentations were over!

"A common mistake if you're suffering from a lack of confidence is to imagine all the things that could possibly go wrong. You need to visualise what you want to happen, not what you don't want to happen. Your subconscious mind doesn't notice a negative. For instance 'don't drop this' becomes 'drop this' to your subconscious," Kyra continued. "When you think of what you *don't want to happen*, your subconscious mind thinks that *is what's happening*. You don't want your mind to start basing your life on those negative experiences. So don't let those negative thoughts go on in your head.

Stop them before they get started! Focus on how you want things to be and, very quickly, you'll notice the positive difference in your life."

In his notes, Matt wrote:

> *Important:*
>
> *STOP yourself from saying:*
> *I'll never be able to ...*
> *I'm no good at ...*
> *They won't like this ...*
> *They'll probably think I'm stupid ...*
>
> *START saying:*
> *I'll give this a go ...*
> *I've done something similar before ...*
> *They might like this ...*
> *I'll ask. Someone else may be wondering the same as I am ...*

Even when the situation has a negative element, Kyra pointed out that it can be phrased in a positive way. "Watch your language," she said. "Your words are every bit as important as your body language. Choose them carefully."

Matt wrote:

> • *positive language – certainly, absolutely, definitely, great, fantastic.*

- *neutral language – hopefully, I'll try, I'll have a go, we might, possibly, it's okay, I'm all right, not too bad.*
- *negative language – no, definitely not, no way, things are horrendous, it's a nightmare at the moment, I can't because . . .*

"Often we stay neutral because we don't want to upset anybody and we don't want to 'over-promise and under-deliver'. We think neutral language is safer. The downside is, neutral language doesn't instil confidence in anybody! Eliminate it!"

Matt looked at the list of neutral language and realised just how often he used it – especially "not too bad" when people asked him how he was in the morning.

"If someone says, 'I'll try to get you the report by Friday' or 'I'll get you the report by lunchtime on Friday', which answer gives you the most confidence in getting the report? Neutral language can make you seem uncertain. Positive language can convey the strength, reliability and confidence you really want to express. And if you can't get it done, or it's dependent on something else happening, say so, with your reasons why."

Tips for Confidence
- Listen to and monitor your own language.
- Cut out the neutral language.
- Be definite. Say what you mean and mean what you say.

Be yourself within your own limitations

Kyra came closer to the audience and lowered her voice, as if she were taking them into her confidence. "Here's something we never talk about," she said, glancing back over her shoulder for dramatic effect, as if someone were listening in. "We all talk about achieving excellence and living in the fast lane. But let's be honest, in the big scheme of things, does it matter if you're as fast as other people or not? We all feel pressured to hurry and keep pace, but in reality, it's a pretty rare occasion for the most part. You can have every reason to be confident, even if you're not the fastest or the strongest or even the sharpest knife in the drawer! The important thing – the truly essential thing – is to be confident in who you are, within your own limitations.

"Suppose I decide I want to be an underwater swimmer. At the beginning, I know I don't like to put my head under water, so this is going to be a challenge for me, because, at the moment, I can't do it. I actually hate swimming under water. Would it really contribute to my life if I could swim under water? Absolutely not. So you'd assume that I'd have no incentive whatever to learn to swim under water. Why should I do it then? Just to push out the limits of what I can do? Sometimes this is reason enough, but maybe there are better ways to do that?

"So much of my business, these days, relies on computers and the internet," Kyra said. "I'm always contacting people through email and referencing websites. If I wanted to arbitrarily push myself into a new arena, wouldn't it make more sense to learn a new computer skill to help me with my work, than to learn how to get comfortable putting my head under water?

"Last year, I took horse riding lessons. I could've taken riding lessons at any point in my life, but I never did. I have no particular interest in horses and no reason to think I'd have any natural skill for riding a horse. But it wasn't just a random way to challenge myself. I chose to take lessons last May because I was going to Mongolia in the summer; we were going to be riding horses for part of our journey, so I wanted to be prepared.

"It's important to look at why you want to do something – even learning a new skill. It's easy for us to spend too much time trying to improve ourselves so we can be perfect, instead of focusing on accepting ourselves within our limitations.

"I hate to break it to you," Kyra smiled. "But you're never going to be perfect, no matter how hard you try! And neither am I. The best any of us can do is keep thinking positively and build our confidence in every way we can."

Matt felt inspired by Kyra's advice. People always talk about thinking positively, of course, but until now, Matt had never had any pressing reason to put it into effect. Having the pressure of this new job and these important presentations had brought a lot of things to his attention that he'd never taken seriously before. All in all, Kyra had given them ten steps for boosting confidence:

1. Take slow, deep breaths.
2. Stand tall and be aware of your posture.
3. Put a smile on your face.

4. Think the right thoughts.
5. Choose your words.
6. Make a confident first impression.
7. Dress for success.
8. Adopt a role.
9. Act as if . . .
10. Visualise what you want to happen.

Looking them over, Matt realised he'd learned to see each one of these steps from a new perspective. When he'd read the list at the beginning of the workshop, he hadn't realised the implications. He would even have said he'd mastered some of these already or they weren't that important. Although most of these steps seemed easy, he could definitely see now how important they were.

Lessons

Matt couldn't wait to get started on the Brick Wall Confidence Builder. He might even go so far as to paste little slips of paper all over his refrigerator. The list of his own bricks was already growing in his mind.

How he wished he'd known all this information when he went to his first presentation! Matt started to berate himself for not doing things right, now that he knew what he should have done differently. Then he realised that berating himself was a classic case of negative thinking!

Think the right thoughts, he reminded himself. *You are never going to be perfect. No matter how hard you try, the things you do could always be improved. So don't even choose that standard for yourself in the first place. It sets you up for failure. The Millcreek presentation was a fiasco, but you've still got one more coming up. Focus on your gratitude and appreciation that you've learned these things before the second presentation.*

That's when Matt realised how many bricks of confidence he could create out of the Millcreek situation: *I can be proud of myself for taking on the project manager job in the first place. I could have stayed safely in my comfort zone, but I was willing to branch out – and risk failure and embarrassment. Now that I've experienced some failure and embarrassment, it hurts a bit, but the good news is, it turns out I can take it. I didn't crumble. I picked myself back up and took action to do better the next time. I sought out good advice from James and Vicki. I took this workshop. That one failure opened the door to new things I could never have imagined before!*

Matt really liked this way of re-framing his experience. Already he was feeling encouraged. He could see how productive and motivating it would be as a way of life. What else could he pull from his experience with Millcreek to strengthen his resolve and future success?

I guess I'm also proud of myself for keeping an open mind at this workshop. I might've come in smugly, assuming I knew more than she did. (Well, actually, I did do that. But I'm proud that I quickly gave it up!) Even though it was challenging for me to recognise that some of my long-term beliefs were wrong or misguided, I was big enough to admit that and see things in a new way.

> **What lies behind us and what lies before us are tiny matters compared to what lies within us.**
> *~ Ralph Waldo Emerson*

All these positive aspects of his experience would have been hidden from him in the past, while he looked for ways to put himself down for the loss of the Millcreek account. He would have felt he "deserved to feel bad about it" and that if he had looked for the good in the experience, he would have been merely trying to find a way to minimise his mistakes or make excuses for himself.

After Kyra's presentation, he realised that his old way of thinking was not as productive as the way she suggested. It was far better to find positive, empowering ways to cope with defeat or disappointment.

Matt felt a new level of confidence starting to take hold inside of him. The effect was much more global than he'd expected. He was not only feeling better about the Millcreek experience, but he was feeling good about his ability to be a project manager, as well.

If he could put these new skills into practice, then he could be much bolder in trying new things, because his defeats would only be stepping stones to new learning and growth. This positive thinking was actually a way to reduce the risk of failure, by turning failure into something useful. It meant that failure did not have to derail you. It could propel you even faster toward your goals! It was a very exciting idea.

Maybe this positive approach would help him take his connection with Vicki to the next level too. Once he'd started noticing his thoughts, it hadn't taken long for him to realise that his mind returned to her again and again. Instinctively, Matt sensed that confidence and positive thinking were about to have a beneficial effect on every area of his life. As Matt read over his notes in preparation for his mentoring meeting with James, he felt a smile ease across his face.

- *Make your first impression a confident one.*
- *You never get a second chance to make a first impression.*
- *Convey confidence with your handshake.*
- *Meet people's eyes and smile.*
- *Create your own confidence using the wall and review it when you feel down!*
- *Visualise the experience you want. Spend time each day imagining things going well.*

- Remember to watch your language. Choose your words carefully.
- Eliminate neutral language. Be definite. Say what you mean and mean what you say.
- Be yourself within your own limitations.
- Avoid false expectations that cannot be met by realising you are never going to be perfect, no matter how hard you try!

Chapter 10

Communication Comes Together

Talking it over with Vicki

As he left the workshop, Matt checked his watch. It was evening in Cambridge, but for Vicki it was still the middle of the afternoon. Matt smiled as he dialled her number. *Sometimes time zones could really work in your favour!*

"Do you have time to talk?" Matt asked, when Vicki said hello. "I've just finished the Kyra Radcliffe seminar."

There was a pause on the other end of the line. Even though he was still brimming with excitement about his experience, he could tell something was wrong.

"Um, yes," Vicki said. "I'm just having a late lunch at my desk. So if you don't mind the sound of lettuce being crunched in the background, go ahead."

Matt noticed a distance in her voice that he hadn't heard before. "Are you sure?"

Vicki cleared her throat. He could hear the squeaking of the chair as she sat up straight. "No, it's fine. I'm eager to hear what happened. Did you enjoy it? Was it worth your time? I know you were ambivalent about going."

"Absolutely!" Matt exclaimed. Whatever was going on with Vicki, it must have been unrelated. He pushed her initial hesitation out of his mind and launched into the discussion. As quickly as he could, Matt reviewed the highlights of the workshop with Vicki. She seemed to warm to the conversation as he went along, making more exclamations and sounds of agreement as he spoke.

"My friend Rosalind used that Brick Wall of Confidence too," Vicki told him. The reluctance had completely vanished from her voice. "She said it made a huge difference. Since she was a girl in school, she felt like she'd remembered every negative thing her teachers or parents had said about her. They were like a tape, constantly running in her head, when she was feeling low or doubting herself.

"At the very moments she needed to encourage herself, she'd hear these negative comments instead: 'I'm no good at this' or 'I'm no good at that'. Then somewhere (maybe from one of Kyra Radcliffe's books), she read about the Brick Wall. It started out small – a few pleasant things on a couple of bricks: 'I always smile and say hello', 'I'm a good neighbour', 'I'm a good friend', 'I make a great shepherd's pie'. Things like that. And after reading that over every morning for a couple of days, it cheered her up so much that she decided to take it further."

"What did she do?" Matt asked.

"She got a huge piece of brown paper and put it on the fridge! Then she took a big black marker and covered the paper with dozens of little blank squares, waiting to be filled in." Vicki laughed a little, remembering it. "Rosalind always has such nerve! I don't know that I'd make it so public that anyone who came into my kitchen could walk up and take a look and laugh at it! But Rosalind didn't mind.

"Dangling down from a pink refrigerator magnet was a piece of brightly coloured yarn with a bright red marker attached to the end. She stuck that to the fridge, on top of her Brick Wall of Confidence. Then, every day – I mean *every day* – she faithfully added one new thing to a brick:

152

I'm always on time for work.
I'm friendly.
I show people I care.
I have a good singing voice.
I'm great with children.
I'm good with figures.
I have beautiful teeth.
I love my hair.
I'm good with clients.
I'm creative.
I'm warm.
I love cats.
I'm a people person.
I'm happy.
I apologise if I'm wrong.
I can admit I'm wrong.
I make a contribution when I can.
I work to improve myself.
I dream in colour."

"How long did it take her to fill it in?" Matt asked, in wonder.

"Months!" Vicki said. "She just kept doing it and, before she knew it, the entire refrigerator was covered in this beautiful, indestructible Brick Wall of Confidence. She actually had a few of us over to celebrate. We had a little appreciation party – for Rosalind, but also to acknowledge ourselves. We spent the evening laughing and talking about things we liked about ourselves and ridiculous things we worried about too. It's surprising how many negative ideas sound so serious and depressing in your own head, but sound completely ridiculous when you tell a friend who loves you."

"What do you mean?"

"Well, one of mine, for instance, was that whenever I doubted myself, I'd say, 'You're a loser!'"

Matt chuckled on the other end of the line. He'd heard that one in his own head.

"That's exactly the way my girlfriends reacted that night, when we were confessing our worst negative thoughts to each other. I said mine was 'I'm a loser' and they laughed!"

"Because they've thought the same thing about themselves," Matt said. "I'll bet everybody's worried about that at some point."

"Yes," Vicki said. "And it was also because I'm not a loser. It's silly for me to say so. I'm not going to be winning the Nobel Prize any time soon, but I've achieved a lot of things in my life that I'm proud of. My accomplishments speak for themselves. Even at my darkest hour, there's no justification for believing I'm a hopeless failure, but that's what negative thoughts are like. Silly ideas, charged with emotion, so they feel absolutely true. But they're not."

Matt thought how much he liked and admired Vicki. "Of course they're not," he said. "You're one of the most interesting people I know."

"*Interesting?*" Vicki moaned. "Oh no, that can't be good!"

Since Matt had been trying to praise her, he was confused. "What's wrong with 'interesting'? Don't you want to be interesting?"

"'Interesting' is what men say about women they don't want to go out with," Vicki told him.

Matt was starting to see where she was coming from, but he knew he wasn't quite up to speed yet, so he stalled for time. "Men only want to go out with women who are boring?"

"Apparently!" Vicki laughed.

"Well, I *definitely* want to go out with you, so what should I have said?"

"Saying you definitely want to go out is a good start," Vicki smiled. "So why don't you want to see me when I come to London?"

Matt was startled. "What do you mean?"

"When I said I was coming to visit my brother, you might've asked to see me . . ."

"Well, I . . . uhm . . ." Now that she mentioned it, Matt couldn't understand why he hadn't asked to see her. Maybe he'd been preoccupied with the presentation when she mentioned it or he'd assumed she would only be coming for her brother's party. He couldn't really explain it – to Vicki or to himself. The only thing he knew, with growing certainty, was that he wanted to see her.

"*If* you were interested, that is . . ." Vicki added, playfully.

"So when can I see you?" Matt asked.

Very quickly, they found themselves making plans to meet in person for the first time. He had experienced a lot of highs and lows over the past few weeks and Vicki had been there through all of them. The idea of finally meeting her made him very happy.

Communicating effectively

Soon he'd be giving the second presentation. His team had worked so hard to bring the projections and graphs together that he was sure the PowerPoint presentation would be even stronger than last time.

A few days ago, when he was at the Reeds' house, he'd had a conversation with Brigit that helped him think about his responsibilities to his team in a new way. "I'm starting to realise that this really isn't something I have to do alone," Matt told her. "My team is there to help me."

"As I've told you all along!" Brigit grinned and nudged his shoulder, teasing him.

"I'm a little slow," Matt smiled.

"A little stubborn, you mean!" Brigit laughed.

"Well, the point is, I finally get it. My team is vital. With this second presentation coming, their input is even more important to me. I want to let them know I appreciate their work and take them into my confidence."

"So what's the problem?" Brigit asked.

"I'm not quite sure how to strike the right balance between friendliness and authority," Matt sighed. "I know it sounds ridiculous, but sometimes I find it hard to know how to talk to them!"

"That doesn't sound ridiculous," Brigit said. "How you speak to your team is so important, when you're in management. Before I was in a management position, I had some bad experiences with it myself."

"You mean that guy with the hair gel who kept asking you out?"

"No, not that guy!" Brigit howled. "But thanks for reminding me. I meant the job at Genera Subsidiaries."

"That place by the bank?"

"Yes. I was in a junior position, so I was basically expected to do whatever I was asked. If a manager isn't conscientious about how they make requests, they can easily sound insulting and condescending."

"In what way?"

"I once had a manager say something like, 'Brigit, darling, would you go and get me that file?'"

"And you felt insulted because he called you 'darling'?"

"It wasn't appropriate. I said, 'I'll go and get it for you, but I am not your darling,'" Brigit said. "That boundary was essential in the workplace. It's really important to me."

"What was his reaction?"

"Well, I was worried about that!" Brigit laughed. "After I got the file for him, I thought, 'Oh my gosh, I shouldn't have spoken to him like that! Whatever did I say that for?' But it was fine. He never spoke to me like that again – even though I heard him speak to other women in the office in that way."

"He knew you wouldn't tolerate it," Matt smiled.

"The nice thing was, I found out I wouldn't tolerate it as well! I guess you don't always know what your boundaries are until they're pushed."

> **He who does not have the courage to speak up for his rights cannot earn the respect of others.**
> ~ *Rene G. Torres*

Thinking it over, Matt was relieved to find he wasn't prone to calling anyone on his team "darling", but he might easily do something else offensive and inappropriate without realising it. "It must be harder for women in a work environment – especially when they're subordinates."

"Unfortunately, this kind of thing continues all the way up the line," Brigit said. "It's one of the reasons I've completely stopped using this term 'subordinate'. The word itself implies separation and superiority."

"What do you say instead?"

"I don't always manage but, as much as possible, I try to refer to my staff as my 'team' or colleagues, or if it's an individual, I use their name."

"I like those better too," Matt said.

"It's what we'd prefer to be called ourselves, isn't it?" Brigit shrugged.

"Yes, it is."

"When I first joined a management team, all the managers sat around a huge table every Friday for a meeting. There were eight to ten of us. I was literally the new kid on the block, and the only woman sitting at a table of men in suits and ties. A very intimidating environment. I was so nervous that when I sat down, I had to stop myself from asking if it was 'okay to sit in this seat'!"

"Funny, that's exactly how I felt at my first meeting with upper management," Matt said.

"At the next week's meeting I sat in the same seat because I thought, 'Well, I know this seat is okay. No-one said anything about it last time.' The senior manager took the seat at the head of the table. But when the No. 2 manager came in, he slid out the chair next to mine and said, 'I'll sit next to the crumpet in the room'!"

"You're kidding! I don't remember you telling me this!"

"I meant to tell you, but I think it happened while you were away on that skiing trip with Paige. I must've forgotten to mention it."

"I can't believe he called you 'crumpet'!"

"Even more amazing, he said it with eight other managers present. No-one said a word."

"Unbelievable," Matt said. "Even I would know better than to say something like that. What did you do?"

"Well, I was sitting there steaming. It was such a demeaning, sexist remark. I was going to say something, but I was afraid I'd burst into tears and make it worse, because my emotions were so high. So I said nothing during the meeting. But I knew myself enough to know I couldn't go home without saying anything.

"After the meeting, I went to speak to his secretary and explained the situation. 'How do you think I should deal with him?' I asked. And she said, 'Why don't you go in and talk to him now?' So I did."

"You must've been scared," Matt said.

"I was nervous, but I knew I had to say something. So I said, 'When you called me a crumpet, I felt it was very inappropriate. I may be a junior manager, but I deserve to be treated with respect.'

"He looked surprised and said, 'Oh, I'm sorry. I didn't mean anything by it.' And I said, 'Well, I'd appreciate it if you didn't call me that again.'"

"Did he?" Matt asked.

"No, he didn't. We had what I felt was a healthy level of respect for each other from that time on."

"That's the kind of respect I want my team to feel," Matt said. "I hope I can help create that kind of environment."

"They know you're on a learning curve," Brigit said, kindly. "As long as you show them you're trying and willing to keep improving, most people will cut some slack. Who knows? They might even give you tips!" she laughed.

Matt laughed too. "I can use all the tips I can get at this point!"

After attending the workshop and spending so much invaluable time talking to James and Vicki, Matt had learned so much. Brigit and Brad had given him great insights too. Even if he didn't get the new account, he was certain that he'd be able to put some of this new knowledge to good use. And he knew that was a start.

With positive thinking and a willingness to learn from his mistakes, he could at least bring confidence and expertise to the presentation.

Getting it right

"You've all done a great job," he told his team before he left for the presentation. "It's going to make a real difference."

"Do you have the adaptor for the projector, in case you need it?" Amy asked, checking the briefcase.

"It's in there," Matt said.

"We're all with you," Steve said, patting him on the back.

"That's right," Justin said. "This is the one that counts. We know you can do it."

"Thanks," Matt said. "Let's go, Amy."

On this presentation, Adrian was not coming with him. After listening to Kyra talk about negative thinking, Matt had realised that Adrian's negative expectations were a real liability. He told Adrian he'd prefer to have one of his own team members along, so he could have back-up on some of the data on the graphs. When he told him that Amy was good with people and would be a real asset on the human relations end as well, Adrian had reluctantly agreed. Matt also felt it would boost Amy's confidence, showing how much he valued her expertise.

When they were in the car, Matt looked at Amy and said, "I'm glad you're coming along. Justin's right. This *is* the one that counts. If we can get this client, it may not save the department, but James said it may well give them confidence that we have *the ability* to save it."

"What does that mean, exactly?" Amy asked.

Matt smiled to realise she was asking for clarification even now. He was glad she was starting to feel more comfortable doing it. "It means that, if we get this right, they may give us another chance."

Amy beamed. "Oh, I hope so! The idea of job hunting fills me with dread."

"I know what you mean," Matt sighed. "I don't want to do that either. So, let's get it right!"

The drive to Thegran was a short one. It was a small firm that had been based in the UK for years. Matt had often passed it on his bicycle during university days and wondered what it was like inside. The old brick building had a large atrium on the roof that let the light in. Matt had always pictured brilliant rays of sunlight pouring through the glass, but, of course, grey, misty light was much more likely.

Instead of being greeted by a series of officious employees, Matt and Amy were warmly welcomed by Carlton Banks, grandson of Paul Banks, who had founded the company. "Welcome to Thegran," he said, extending his hand to Matt.

Carlton's relaxed manner immediately put Matt at ease. By the time they had settled into the conference room for the presentation, Matt was already talking to Carlton about elements of the presentation in a very casual and engaging way. As Carlton asked interested questions, all of the information seemed to flow very naturally.

Whenever he started to doubt himself or feel self-conscious, Matt remembered what Kyra Radcliffe had said about adopting a role. "I'm a confident, knowledgeable advocate for our company," he told himself. "This presentation is going to go well." Positive reinforcement kept him in a confident frame of mind, so it was easier to look people in the eyes and speak clearly. When he noticed how confident his voice sounded, that gave his confidence a little boost as well.

Within minutes, Thegran's Director of Operators had joined Matt and Amy around the conference table. He had specific questions about growth projections and quality reports. Matt and Amy glanced at one another with pleased smiles when they realised that these two men were asking for exactly the information they'd spent hours collecting and preparing for this presentation. Everything was working – even better than they'd hoped!

After almost thirty minutes of conversation, Matt easily introduced the visuals. "Amy and the rest of the team have prepared some graphics to make this clearer. Would you like to see them?" He opened the laptop and turned it toward them.

"Of course," they said, leaning forward to see the PowerPoint display.

While they were looking at the first PowerPoint presentation page, Matt consciously relaxed his shoulders and took a few deep, steady breaths. Kyra was right. He hadn't felt very tense – especially not compared to how he'd felt during his first presentation – but the deliberate effort to relax seemed to ground him and make him even more sure of himself.

Matt marvelled at how smoothly it was going. When he reached the end, he expected them to thank him and say they'd think things over, but Carlton shook his hand. "Cambridge Enterprise & Design sounds like it has exactly the solutions we're looking for," he said. "I have no hesitation whatsoever. We'd be glad to work with you."

When they got to the car park, Matt sent a quick text to Vicki to let her know. He couldn't wait to share his excitement.

> We got it right!
> Sweet Success!!!
> ~ Matt

A victory lap

When Matt and Amy got back to the office, they were grinning so widely that everyone who saw them knew how well it had gone. Justin and Steve jumped up from their desks.

"How good was it?" Justin asked.

"It was fantastic!" Matt grinned.

"He was amazing," Amy told them. "He was so confident and positive. He answered their questions and gave them all our data as if it was the most natural thing in the world."

"So, really, it was our data that made the difference," Steve smiled.

"Yes, it was," Matt agreed. "We had exactly the right information to answer their questions. You guys are brilliant."

"It sounds like congratulations are in order," Adrian said, watching them from the doorway of his office.

Matt crossed the room to give Adrian Carlton's business card and contact information. "It went very well," he said. "They'd like to talk with you about the long-term possibilities."

It was a rare thing to see, but Adrian actually smiled. "It seems to be your lucky day," he said. "While you were gone, I just received a call from Millcreek."

Matt exchanged glances with the team. At the very mention of the name Millcreek, a look of tension had come over their faces. "What did they want?"

"They said they've experienced problems in their negotiations with the company that was supposed to take our place. Something about poor quality control and lack of professionalism." Adrian looked pleased and smug. "They've cancelled that contract and want to renew with us."

Everyone cried out at once. Steve and Amy started laughing and cheering. Justin strode over to Matt and proudly shook his hand.

"Looks like your department is saved," Adrian said.

The acknowledgement from Adrian was especially sweet. Matt had sometimes felt they were adversaries, but Adrian's congratulations felt genuine. Whatever doubts he may have about Matt as a project manager, he was able to share this moment of success with the team. Matt was grateful for that.

A few minutes later, James came to join them. He put a fatherly hand on Matt's shoulder and said, "Good job, Matt. I knew you could do it."

For the first time, Matt felt he was really starting to come into his own.

Covent Garden

When Matt went to London to meet Vicki for a glass of wine in Covent Garden, he had no trouble thinking positively or feeling confident. He knew she wanted to meet him as much as he wanted to meet her. Yet his feeling of anxiety was almost overwhelming. Kyra Radcliffe hadn't talked about this! What do you do with a feeling of such happy anticipation? *Play it cool*, he told himself, but that only worked for a few seconds at a time. He thought of adopting a role, but didn't think that would be appropriate for this situation either. He wanted to be himself around Vicki. Yet he couldn't stop his mind from racing.

When he finally saw her crossing the square, everything changed. She looked exactly as he thought she'd look. All of his anxiety faded as he walked towards her, smiling. There was no need for anxiety. This was a woman he already knew well and respected – maybe a woman he would come to love.

Lessons

Matt knew he'd come a long way in a short period of time. Looking back, he was surprised to realise how much he'd learned. If things went well with Vicki, his life might change even more dramatically in the months ahead. When he looked back over the lessons that had had the greatest impact on his life, he noticed that many of them had to do with treating the people around him with consideration and respect.

In order to treat others well, he had to come from a place of poise and confidence within himself. Putting these lessons into practice had not only made him a better project manager, they had improved the quality of his life – at the office and at home. He was grateful for the support he had received from people around him, as he'd stumbled along, trying to learn these skills. It made him want to give back, by passing that goodwill and support along to others. Personal relationships may have turned out to be a lot more complicated than he'd expected, but they were a lot more rewarding as well.

- Generate a respectful atmosphere by treating your staff as individuals, not 'subordinates'. Use their names. Refer to them as a 'team' or as 'colleagues'.
- Always show your gratitude for work well done.
- Stand up for yourself and your rights – remembering to respect the rights of others.
- Enlist the help of friends and colleagues – don't try to do it all alone. If you need help, ask.
- You can learn something new if you keep an open mind.
- Visualise successful outcomes – and they may even come to be real.
- Thinking positively really does work!

Further Reading

Personal Development

Frankl, V.E., 1984: *Man's Search for Meaning* (Washington Square Press)

(A small book with a very powerful message about our own self worth – based on his experiences in the concentration camps.)

Jeffers, S., 1991: *Feel the Fear and do it Anyway* (Arrow Books)

(A great little book, which is easy to read. It gives a good introduction into building confidence.)

Loer, J. and Schwartz, T., 2003: *On Form: Achieving High Energy Performance Without Sacrificing Health and Happiness and Life Balance* (Nicholas Brealey Publishing)

(Strategies for managing your energy and improving performance.)

Seligman, M., Ph.D, 2003: *Authentic Happiness* (Nicholas Brealey Publishing)

(Takes recent science psychology and applies it to the fundamental question of happiness.)

Neuro-linguistic Programming (NLP)

There are lots of books on this subject – here are a couple of my favourites:

Charvet, S.R., 1997: *Words that Change Minds* (Kendall/Hunt Publishing Company)

(A more in-depth book, very practical. For those of you who want to learn more, Shelle has a fabulous sense of humour and occasionally comes to the UK to run some great courses.)

O'Connor, J. and McDermott, I., 1996: *Principles of NLP* (Thorsons)

(A basic introduction into NLP, comprehensive and readable.)

Energy and Well-being

Feinstein, D., Eden, D. and Craig, G., 2005: *The Promise of Energy Psychology* (Jeremy P. Tarcher/The Penguin Group)
(This book combines the latest scientific research, with the principles of energy medicine and Emotional Freedom Techniques (EFT))

Sapolsky, R.M., 1998: *Why Zebras Don't Get Ulcers* (W.H. Freeman and Company)
(A fascinating read on stress and how our bodies react – good scientific basis.)

Further personal/leadership development organisations

Junior Chamber International (UK) www.jciuk.org.uk
Junior Chamber International (Worldwide) www.jci.cc
Toastmasters International www.toastmasters.org

About the Author

Kate Atkin grew up on her father's arable farm in Lincolnshire where she spent weekends and holidays working on the farm.

After the death of her elder sister in 1989, she left her management job at Barclays Bank to backpack around Australia and New Zealand. Travelling alone over those months, Kate learnt to expect the unexpected and found reserves of inner strength and confidence that she never realised she possessed.

As an inspirational speaker and expert facilitator Kate has presented at conferences in North America and Europe as well as around the UK. She won the 2007 UK & Ireland Speech Evaluation Contest run by Toastmasters International and was recognised as the Most Outstanding Trainer by Junior Chamber International UK in 2005. Kate is also a World Debating Champion.

Kate is a supportive and inspiring individual with high levels of energy, drive and passion. In her speaking, training and coaching she acts as a catalyst for change, instils self-belief and encourages delegates to listen to their inner voices. She also shares her personal experiences, bringing theory to life. Kate challenges assumptions and uses theories in a practical way to help individuals, teams and organisations increase their communication and performance. For Kate the personal touch is essential.

Kate holds a master's degree in Applied Positive Psychology and is a regular speaker on the mindset needed to generate confidence and how to flourish at work and in life. She works with companies and individuals who wish to bring about positive change.

In the writing of this book Kate has drawn upon the experiences of her colleagues and delegates as well as her own management experience to ensure that the challenges encountered and lessons learnt by the characters are realistic. However, any similarities with living persons are purely accidental, with the exception of Kyra Radcliff, who is largely modelled on herself.

Kate Atkin focuses on personal and organisational development through coaching, facilitation, speaking and training. Kate is based in Cambridge and operates throughout the UK and internationally.

Coaching

Through coaching you will be listened to, have your thinking challenged and be encouraged to identify ways of moving forward and to take action.

Facilitation

As a facilitator Kate's approach is to identify key issues and encourage discussion and understanding and to ensure clear outcomes are obtained from the meetings. Typically Kate is called upon to facilitate meetings in-house between groups who have communication difficulties or externally to gather viewpoints from a wide variety of representatives.

Speaking

As a professional speaker Kate inspires her audience through personal examples and encourages debate. Both motivating and thought provoking Kate inspires her audiences to fully participate and to leave with practical ways of making a positive difference.

Training

An enthusiastic, engaging and knowledgeable trainer, Kate employs accelerated learning techniques in her courses to ensure information is taken away and applied back in the workplace. She sees training not as something that is done, but rather as learning which is participatory.

To find out more about the services and courses offered please get in touch:

Kate Atkin
Aspire 2
St John's Innovation Centre
Cowley Road
Cambridge
CB4 0WS

Telephone: +44 (0) 7779 646 976

www.kateatkin.com
kate@kateatkin.com